·West Coast· Seafood Recipes

Blaine Freer

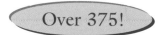

Over 375!

Easy-to-Prepare Seafood Recipes for Two People

Illustrations by Dürten Kampmann

Frank Amato
PORTLAND

A c k n o w l e d g m e n t s

If there is anything completely beyond measure, other than the limits of space itself, it's the infinite variety in which food can be prepared. In almost any newspaper, in many magazines and television programs, as well as on canned and packaged foods, a seemingly endless number of recipes come streaming forth from countless kitchens.

This book, it must be stated at the outset, is not intended as a breakthrough to a new plateau of the culinary art. Rather, it's a gathering between two covers of seafood recipes which originally came from a great many sources but which have been revised, for the most part, to meet the following requirements:

1. The recipes are designed for two persons with a minimum of leftovers.

2. They require as short a list of ingredients as possible, and use only those ingredients which may be readily obtained from your neighborhood supermarket or delicatessen.

3. Measurements and directions have been standardized throughout for ease in preparation

If there is an innovation it would be the inclusion of the three numbered boxes with each recipe to aid in giving it a rating. They also serve as a reminder as to whether or not you had previously used the recipe.

Most of the recipes were inspired by those found in a variety of sources, but changed in varying degrees to meet the book's theme of cooking for two persons. We nevertheless acknowledge our debt to the unknown host of cooks whose recipes have been altered, but which in their original state have made such an enormous contribution to the versatile cuisine which is ours to enjoy.

We also wish to thank Brown Eyes for her willingness to clean up the kitchen on numberless occasions. And we also extend thanks to our springer spaniel, Patty, whose uncritical palate so enthusiastically placed the stamp of approval on every dish presented for her appraisal.

Published in 1995 by Frank Amato Publications, Inc.
P.O. Box 82112, Portland, Oregon 97282
(503) 653-8108
Line drawings: Durten Kampmann
Softbound ISBN: 1-57188-046-1   Softbound UPC: 0-66066-00242-6
Book Design: Tony Amato
Printed in Hong Kong
3 5 7 9 10 8 6 4

Table of Contents

Calorie Counter

Seafood, prepared in the infinite variety to which it lends itself, is delicious. However, its popularity goes well beyond the pleasure it affords at the table. In an increasingly health-conscious world, it also offers excellent nutrition with low calorie and cholesterol counts.

As an aid to calorie-counters, the total number of calories is listed with each recipe.

And, for your further information, following is a table showing the calorie content of most of the ingredients used. Although it's impossible to calculate the calories found in each recipe with absolute and unvarying precision, an average is struck so the final tally is accurate to a very reasonable degree.

The following table may also be used to aid in making calculations of the calorie content of recipes not included in this book. Most of the ingredients listed are commonly found in seafood recipes.

SEAFOOD	CALORIES
Albacore (50 per oz.), 1 lb..........800	Salmon (sockeye) 3 1/2-oz. can.......185
Anchovies (five)..................25	Salmon (pink) 7 3/4-oz. can..........310
Clams, canned, 6 1/2 oz............133	Salmon (pink) 15 1/2-oz. can.........620
Clams, raw, 1 cup.................160	Salmon (king/coho) steak or fillet......800
Crabmeat, canned, 6 oz............125	Scallops, 1 lb.....................50
Halibut steak or fillet, 1 lb..........480	Shrimp, 4 1/2-oz. can, drained........150
Oysters, raw, 1 cup, 220; 10 oz.......270	Smelt, 1 oz.......................30
Rockfish fillet, 1 lb................480	Squid, l lb.......................480
Rockfish, flaked, 1 cup.............250	Tnaa, oil-packed, 3 1/2 oz. can.......197
Sablefish (black cod) 1 lb...........800	Tuna, water-packed, 3 1/2 oz. can.....120
Salmon (pink) 3 1/2 oz.-can.........140	Tuna, water-packed, 7 1/2 oz. can.....220
	Tuna, water-packed, 12 1/2 oz. can....425

NOTE: Most of the white-meated fish bought at the market is some species of rockfish and will be rated at 30 calories per ounce. Trout will be rated at 50 calories per ouce.

OTHER INGREDIENTS	CALORIES
Almonds, slivered, 1/2 cup..........285	Bread, whole wheat, 1 slice..........55
Apple, 1 medium (2 1/2 in. diameter)..70	Bread, white, 1 slice................65
Asparagus, 6 medium...............20	Bread, fresh crumbs (1 slice = 1 cup)...65
Asparagus, frozen, 3.3 oz.-pkg........25	Bread, 1 cup fine dry bread crumbs =
Bacon, 1 slice cooked..............35	4 slices.......................260
Bacon, 1 slice uncooked............90	Broccoli, 1/2 cup..................20
Barbecue sauce, 1 TBsp............25	Buns, hamburger..................120
Beans, green, 1 cup...............50	Butter, 1/4 stick (2 TBsp.)...........200
Beer, 8 oz.......................100	Buttermilk, 1 cup..................90
Bouillon cube, one................5	Cabbage, finely shredded, 1 cup......22
	Carrots, grated or diced, 1 cup........50

Cashews, 1/2 cup. 385
Celery, diced, 1 cup. 20
Cheese, cheddar or American, 1 slice . . 80
Cheese, cheddar or American, 1 oz. 110
Cheese, cream, 1 oz. 100
Cheese, creamed cottage, 1 cup. 260
Cheese, grated cheddar, 1 cup 330
Cheese, Monterey Jack, 1 oz. 110
Cheese, parmesan, 1 TBsp. 33
Chicken broth, 14-oz. can 40
Chicken, white, 2 1/2-oz. can. 100
Chicken, white, without skin, 1/2 cup. . .130
Chicken, white, with skin, 1/2 cup 213
Chili sauce, 1/4 cup 50
Clam chowder, Hilton's cond., 10 1/2-
    oz. can. 150
Clam chowder, Snow's cond., 15-oz. can 280
Clam juice, 1 cup. 20
Corn, whole or cream-style, 1/2 cup. . . .80
Corn, whole or cream-style, 17-oz. can .240
Corn flakes, crushed, 1 cup 110
Crackers, soda, crushed, 24 to 1 cup . . .240
Crackers, Ritz, (9). 150
Crackers, Ritz, 1 cup crushed. 400
Cream, half and half, 1/2 cup. 160
Cream, light, 1/2 cup 249
Cream, heavy, 1/2 cup 440
Cream, sour, 1/2 cup 240
Creamer, non dairy liquid, 1/2 cup. . . .128
Cucumber, peeled, sliced, 1 cup 20
Dressing, French/Italian, 1 TBsp. 70
Eggs, large, whole. 80
Eggs, large, whites only. 20
Flour, all-purpose white, 1/2 cup 200
Flour, all-purpose white, 1 heaping TBsp.50
Flour, baking mix, 1/2 cup 240
Flour, cornmeal, 1 heaping TBsp. 100
Flour, cornmeal, 1/2 cup 400
Gelatin, plain, dry, 1 pkg. 35
Ham, lean, cubed, 1 cup 300
Hollandaise sauce, 1 TBsp. 50
Horseradish, 1 TBsp. 16
Imo, 1/2 cup. 240
Ketchup, 1 TBsp. 15
Lemon, 1 medium 10
Lemon juice (reconstituted) 2 TBsp. 6
Macaroni, 1 cup cooked. 160
Margarine, 1/4 stick 180
Mayonnaise, 1 TBsp. 90
Mayonnaise, 1/2 cup 540

Mayonnaise, lo-cal, 1 TBsp. 45
Mayonnaise, lo-cal, 1/2 cup. 270
Milk, whole, 3.5% fat, 1 cup 160
Milk, 2% fat, 1 cup. 120
Milk, skimmed, 1 cup. 90
Milk, evaporated, 4 fluid oz. 170
Milk, powdered, 1 cup. 80
Mushrooms, raw, diced, 1 cup. 20
Mushrooms, 4-oz. can 28
Mustard, prepared, 1 TBsp. 10
Noodles, chow mein, 3 oz. 100
Noodles, cooked, 1 cup 200
Oatmeal, 1 cup. 180
Oil, vegetable, 1 TBsp. 90
Okra, 1 cup 45
Olives, ripe, 4-oz. can 100
Olives, stuffed, 4 medium. 20
Onions, raw, diced, 1 cup 45
Orange juice, 6 oz. 85
Peas, canned or frozen, 1/2 cup 60
Pecans, 1/2 cup 370
Peppers, green, diced, 1 cup. 25
Pickles, sliced dill, 1 cup 18
Pickles, sliced sweet, 1 cup 160
Pickle relish, 1 oz. 35
Pimento, 1 oz. 10
Pineapple, crushed or chunks,
    8-oz. can .70
Pineapple, raw, diced, 1 cup 80
Pineapple juice, 6 oz. 100
Pork, salt, 1 oz. 100
Potato buds, 1/2 cup. 139
Potato chips, 10 medium 115
Potatoes, mashed, no butter or milk,
    1/2 cup 60
Potatoes, peeled, diced, 1 cup 100
Raisins, 3 oz. 250
Rice, brown, long-grained, cooked, 1 cup 230
Rice, frozen, 11-oz. pkg. 390
Rice, white enriched, cooked, 1 cup. . . .220
Rice, white, instant, cooked, 1 cup. 180
Rice, instant, uncooked, 1/2 cup. 180
Rolls, dinner (1) 100
Sauerkraut, canned, 1/2 cup. 20
Sausage, pork, 1 oz. 130
Soup, chicken/rice mix, 1 pkg. 50
Soup, cond. chicken/noodle,
    10 3/4-oz. can 191
Soup, condensed, cream-style, 10 3/4-oz. can
    Asparagus 247

Celery 275		Sugar, granulated, 1 cup. 768	
Chicken. 225		Sugar, powdered, 1 level TBsp.. 28	
Clam chowder 210		Sugar, powdered, 1 cup 460	
Green pea 250		Tartar sauce, 1 TBsp. 70	
Mushroom .250		Tomatoes, 17-oz. can. 80	
Potato 192		Tomatoes, raw, 3-inch diameter. 40	
Shrimp 268		Tomatoes, sliced, 1 cup 60	
Tomato. 241		Tomato juice, 1 cup 40	
Soup, cond. vegetable, 10 3/4-oz. can . .102		Tomato paste, 2-oz. can. 45	
Soy sauce, 1 TBsp. 12		Tomato sauce, 8-oz. can. 70	
Spaghetti, 1 cup cooked. 210		Walnuts, chopped, 1/2 cup. 390	
Spaghetti sauce, 4 oz.. 140		Wine, dry, 1/4 cup 50	
Sugar, brown, 1 level TBsp. 51		Worcestershire sauce, 1 TBsp. 10	
Sugar, brown, 1 cup. 816		Yogurt, plain, 1 cup 140	
Sugar, granulated, 1 level TBsp. 48		Zucchini, diced, 1/2 cup. 20	

The above information came from a variety of sources, such as, *A Self-Care Diary for Diabetics* and, *The Brand Name Nutritional Counter*, by Jean Carper, as well as from calorie counts listed on the labels of canned and packaged foods.

Conversions

FLUID MEASUREMENTS

Three teaspoons (tsp.) = one tablespoon (TBsp.)
Two tablespoons = one fluid ounce (oz.)
Four tablespoons = 1/4 cup
Eight ounces (16 tablespoons) = 1 cup
Two cups = one pint
Two pints = one quart
Four quarts = one gallon

DRY MEASUREMENTS

Two heaping tablespoons (as of flour) = 1/4 cup
One pat butter or margarine = 1/2 tablespoon
One tablespoon = 1/8 stick butter or margarine
One stick butter or margarine = 1/4 pound
One stick = 1/2 cup melted
One cup uncooked macaroni = two cups cooked
One cup uncooked rice = two cups cooked
One cup uncooked noodles = 1 1/2 cups cooked
One slice bread = one cup fresh bread crumbs
Four slices bread = one cup fine dry bread crumbs

Substitutions

Margarine for butter
Yogurt or Imo for sour cream
Liquid non-dairy cream for cream or half and half
Egg substitutes for eggs
Lo-cal non-fat mayonnaise for regular mayonnaise

HOW MUCH IS IN A TABLESPOON?

Most recipes call for a tablespoon of this or that. But how much, really, is in a tablespoon? The amount of some sort of liquid in a tablespoon, such as lemon juice or soy sauce, is predictable.

But what about the amount in a tablespoon of a more cohesive ingredient such as flour, for example, or mayonnaise?

To be consistent, all of the instructions in this book calling for a tablespoon, other than liquid, will mean a heaping measure.

Rate the Recipes

Inevitably people react to different recipes in different ways. Almost any individual will favor certain methods of preparation over others.

There are doubtless many occasions when a person, looking over recipes in a well-used cookbook for tonight's supper, won't remember which ones have been used before, or if it was liked well enough to repeat.

This book contains hundreds of recipes, and we hope you follow the suggestions contained herein for many years to come. It's possible you, too, may have a hazy recollection of having used the recipe before, as well as the reactions to it.

As an aid in remembering, a rating chart is included with each recipe. The chart is a simple one. All you need to do is mark an "X" in whatever square is most appropriate.

And, in addition, the total number of calories in each recipe is included, as in the following

❏ 1   ❏ 2   ❏ 3   500 calories

The following words which describe the ratings are merely suggestions. You may supply your own responses.

1. Not so good. This one I can do without.

2. This recipe's pretty good. But I think it could be improved with a little bit more of this, or a smidge less of that.

3. Hey, great! This one's a keeper. If I want to impress someone with my cooking prowess, this is the recipe I'll use.

Foreword

There is an ancient saying which states that, "The Gods do not count against the span of a man's life the time he spends fishing."

Taken at face value one would conclude that, were a person to spend 24 hours a day fishing the year-round, he or she would become immortal. Obviously, such a notion will not be received seriously.

Nevertheless, those fortunates who were to follow the dictates of every recipe in this book, and who were also able to fish for, and catch, every one of the sea creatures necessary, would attain—if not immortality—a degree of satisfaction, fulfilment and good health reserved for very few in this imperfect world.

It could also be charged, certainly with justification, that only a chosen few of the most avid of anglers could catch all of the required seafood. Even so, it would be possible because there's no need to travel the globe to obtain the required fish, such as Africa for a recipe calling for Nile perch, or to South America for an arawana. The sea creatures you'll need, as well as all the other ingredients, will be found at any seafood store, deli or your neighborhood supermarket.

So, you needn't be a fisherperson at all, but rather a person who appreciates the dietary benefits, and the gustatory delights, found in seafood cooking.

❧ 1 ❧

Salmon Steaks and Fillets

Pacific salmon is the undisputed king of Northwest fish, both from the standpoint of its popularity as a table delight and the value placed on it by recreational anglers and commercial interests. Its rich, red flesh and excellent flavor lends itself to a variety of cooking methods, as long as those methods don't detract from the fine flavor of the salmon itself.

Five species return to North American waters—Chinook, coho, sockeye, pink and chum. Although there are differences in the five as to size, color of flesh and oil content, they are sufficiently similar that we won't attempt to designate a particular species to a certain recipe. Suffice it to say that the first two named, Chinook and coho, are more often preferred as steaks or fillets, while the others—especially sockeye and pink—are more likely found in a can.

In season, fresh salmon in the round, in steaks or fillets, is available in supermarkets and seafood stores. A dedicated sports angler will find them legal game in some Northwest waters the year-round.

The difference between a steak and a fillet is in the cutting. A steak is cut across the girth of the salmon leaving a portion of the backbone and a few rib bones in each steak. A fillet is cut along the length of the fish and, in theory at least, is boneless. In oven-cooking a fillet, the skin is often, but not always, removed, but is left on when grilling or smoking.

You may note there are fewer recipes in this chapter than in the chapter for bottomfish fillets. There's a reason. Once when Brown Eyes and I were at Sekiu, near the northwest tip of Washington, we'd gotten up at the pre-dawn hour customary to salmon fisherpersons and were on the water when the sun was evidenced only by a faint glow to the east over the Strait of Juan de Fuca. Fortune favored us, for in time a salmon of 15 pounds, or so, fresh from the ocean, lay in the fish box.

Having departed without breakfast, and with the sun now rising well above the hazy horizon, we headed back to our camper. On this occasion, however, breakfast didn't consist of any such traditional favorites as cereal, hotcakes, bacon, sausage, eggs or hotcakes. Two thick salmon steaks were fried, hot and fast in butter, and the result was a taste delight impossible to achieve by the greatest chefs of Paris. I will not concede that hunger alone prompted that incomparable repast.

On this occasion my opinion was formed that salmon, with its unique and dominant flavor, doesn't require a lot of seasoning, or other ingredients, to improve its palatability. This is especially true if it's been out of the water scarcely more than a couple of hours.

If, however, you want to experiment preparing salmon with more recipes than shown here, just turn to the chapter on bottomfish fillets and use the king of Northwest seafood instead.

No chapter on steelhead is included in these pages because this sea-going rainbow trout is quite similar to salmon. In any event, considering the value of steelhead as a sports-caught fish, along with its threatened status in so many streams, we decline to promote it for any other purpose.

Heat Up the Oven

There is no doubt that a salmon steak, fried in an oiled skillet, is about as conventional a cooking method as you'll find. And, as described in the foregoing, freshly-caught salmon, sizzling in butter or margarine, produces a taste delight difficult to beat. However, the oven offers a wide range of options. For example, try a steak or fillet—

BAKED WITH MAYONNAISE TOPPING

A quick and simple method of baking a salmon steak or fillet is to mix mayonnaise with an equal amount of sour cream or sour cream substitute, plus horseradish. It may be in milder form such as a horseradish sauce, whipped horseradish, or as hot as your heroic taste buds allow. Another suggestion would be to mix the mayonnaise with some type of dry wine.

Simply season the fillet with salt and pepper to your taste, cover with the mayonnaise mixture, place in a greased oven pan and bake 20 to 25 minutes at 350 degrees. An added touch would be to sprinkle the fillet with lemon juice before adding the mayonnaise mixture. If you're in no hurry, after covering the fillet with the mayonnaise mixture, place it in the refrigerator overnight to allow the flavors to penetrate the fish.

But if you're in a REAL big hurry, simply sprinkle the fish with lemon-pepper seasoning, place on a greased oven pan and bake 15 minutes at 400 degrees.

Following are two more simple suggestions using mayonnaise as a base. All of the recipes, by the way, call for 1/2 pound of salmon, but don't feel you're obliged to use this precise amount. Mainly it's an aid in figuring a calorie count.

SUPER BAKE WITH DILL

1/2 lb. steaks or fillets
Salt, pepper and
  onion flakes

4 TBsp. mayonnaise
Onion salt, dill weed,
  lemon juice and paprika

Sprinkle salmon with salt, pepper and onion flakes. Cover with mayonnaise and sprinkle with remaining ingredients. Lay in a greased oven pan and bake 20-25 minutes at 350 degrees.

❏ 1 ❏ 2 ❏ 3   800 calories

SUPER BAKE WITH BROWN SUGAR

1/2 lb. steaks or fillets
Lemon juice, onion powder,
  garlic powder and salt

1/2 cup mayonnaise
4 TBsp. brown sugar

Sprinkle salmon with lemon juice, onion and garlic powder, and salt. Cover with mayonnaise, sprinkle with brown sugar, lay in a greased oven pan and bake 20-25 minutes at 350 deegrees.

❏ 1 ❏ 2 ❏ 3   1,002 calories

Skip the Mayonnaise, but Keep the Oven Hot

CREAMY SALMON BAKE

1/2 lb. steaks or fillets
2 TBsp. diced onion
1 tsp. dill weed
Salt and pepper to taste

1/4 stick margarine
1/2 cup cream or milk
1 TBsp. cornstarch, or as
  needed

Arrange fish in a greased oven pan, sprinkle with onion and seasonings and dot with margarine. Pour cream or milk over all and bake 20-25 minutes at 350 degrees.

Remove steaks from liquid and keep warm. Dissolve a tablespoon of cornstarch in a bit of milk and add to the liquid, heating and stirring until thickened, using as a sauce over the fish.

❏ 1 ❏ 2 ❏ 3   640 calories

VEGGIE SALMON STEAKS

1 tsp. crushed basil
1/2 tsp. salt, or to taste
1/4 tsp. pepper, or to taste
1/4 cup diced green onion

1 can (4 oz.) mushroom pieces
1/2 cup sliced zucchini
1 cubed tomato
1/2 lb. steaks or fillets

After combining seasonings, sprinkle half over vegetables in bottom of a greased oven pan. Lay salmon over veggies, sprinkle with remaining seasonings and bake 20-25 minutes at 350 degrees.

❏ 1 ❏ 2 ❏ 3   459 calories

LEMON/MUSHROOM CUSTARD

1 can (4 oz.) mushroom pieces
2 TBsp. lemon juice
Water as needed
1/4 stick margarine
2 TBsp. flour

1 beaten egg
1 TBsp. onion flakes
Salt and pepper to taste
1/2 lb. steaks or fillets
12 crushed crackers

Drain mushrooms and combine liquid with lemon juice and water to make one cup. In a skillet melt margarine, add flour and gradually stir in liquid until thickened.

Stir in egg, mushrooms, onion and seasonings. Place fish in a greased oven pan, pour sauce over all, top with crushed crackers and bake 20-25 minutes at 350 degrees.

❏ 1 ❏ 2 ❏ 3   858 calories

SMOKY SALMON STEAKS

1/2 lb. steaks or fillets
Salt and pepper to taste
1 can (4 oz.) mushroom pieces

1 tsp. liquid smoke
1/4 cup ketchup
1/4 cup diced green onion

Lay seasoned fish in a greased oven pan, spread over with remaining ingredients and bake 20-25 minutes at 350 degrees.

❏ 1 ❏ 2 ❏ 3   499 calories

CRISPY BAKED SALMON

1/2 lb. steaks or fillets
1/2 cup milk, or as needed
1/2 tsp. salt, or to taste

1 TBsp. lemon juice
Corn flake crumbs as needed
1/4 stick melted margarine

Dip fish in combined milk, salt and lemon juice, roll in corn flakes crumbs, pour over with melted margarine and bake 20-25 minutes at 350 degrees

❏ 1 ❏ 2 ❏ 3   499 calories

CRUNCHY BAKE

6 crushed crackers
2 TBsp. grated parmesan
2 TBsp. chopped nuts
1/2 lb. steaks or fillets

Flour as needed
Salt and pepper to taste
1 beaten egg
2 TBsp. lemon juice
1/4 stick margarine

Combine crackers, cheese and nuts (pecans, walnuts, etc.). Dip seasoned and floured fish in beaten egg, roll in crumb mixture and lay in a greased oven pan.

Combine lemon juice and melted margarine, drizzle over fish and bake 20-25 minutes at 350 degrees.

❏ 1 ❏ 2 ❏ 3   1,085 calories

HERB'S SALMON STEAK

1/4 stick melted margarine
2 TBsp. lemon juice
1/2 tsp. marjoram
1/2 tsp. lemon-pepper

2 TBsp. onion flakes
1/2 lb. steaks or fillets
Salt and pepper to taste
Paprika as desired

Combine margarine with lemon juice, marjoram, lemon-pepper and onion flakes, pour over seasoned salmon and marinate for an hour or so. Lay in a greased oven pan, sprinkle with paprika if desired and bake 20-25 minutes at 350 degrees.

❏ 1 ❏ 2 ❏ 3   580 calories

EVANGELISTA'S FILLETS

1/2 lb. (2) steaks or fillets
Salt and pepper to taste

1/2 cup fine dry bread crumbs
1/4 cup Italian salad dressing
1/4 stick margarine

Lay seasoned salmon in a greased oven pan, cover with bread crumbs and drizzle salad dressing over all. Place tablespoon of margarine on each steak or fillet and bake 20-25 minutes at 350 degrees.

❏ 1 ❏ 2 ❏ 3   990 calories

QUICKIE BARBECUE BAKE

Salt and pepper steaks or fillets to taste, cover with barbecue sauce and bake 20-25 minutes at 350 degrees.

❏ 1 ❏ 2 ❏ 3   990 calories

Get Out the Skillet

SALMON WITH CHICKEN SAUCE

1/2 lb. steaks or fillets	1 cup chicken bouillon
1/2 tsp. garlic powder	2 TBsp. diced green onion
1/2 cup instant potato flakes	1 TBsp. parsley flakes

Poach fish, or cook in microwave, set aside and keep warm.

In a skillet or saucepan heat garlic powder, potato flakes and chicken bouillon, stirring until thickened.

Pour over fish, garnishing with onion and parsley.

❏ 1 ❏ 2 ❏ 3   540 calories

VEGGIE FISH DISH

1/4 stick margarine	1/2 cup sliced zucchini
1/2 cup diced onion	1/2 cup chopped tomatoes
1/2 cup diced celery	2 TBsp. lemon juice
1/2 cup sliced mushrooms, or	1/2 lb. steaks or fillets
1 4-oz. can mushroom pieces	Salt and pepper to taste

In a skillet saute veggies in margarine until tender. Add remaining ingredients, cover and simmer until fish flakes. The kinds and amounts of vegetables can vary.

❏ 1 ❏ 2 ❏ 3   680 calories

FILLETS WITH SOUR CREAM

1/4 stick margarine	1/2 tsp. basil
1/2 lb. steaks or fillets	1/2 cup sour cream
Salt and pepper to taste	Paprika as desired

In a skillet fry fillets until flaky, place on plates and keep warm. In saucepan combine remaining ingredients except paprika, heat as desired, pour over fish and sprinkle with paprika.

❏ 1 ❏ 2 ❏ 3   820 calories

Grilled, Over the Coals with Smoke

One of the tastiest methods of preparing salmon is to grill, or barbecue, over coals on which a hardwood, such as alder or hickory, has been added to create smoke. Fillets with the skin on are recommended over skinless fillets as the skin holds the meat together. Steaks may also be grilled by laying them on aluminum foil, or using a wire basket with a moveable grill which securely holds it together. The basket also makes it possible to turn the salmon over for basting on both sides.

Barbecuing with smoke is obviously done outdoors, preferably using a grill with a hood to hold in the heat and smoke. The fillets are laid on the grill, skin side down, and not turned during the cooking process.

The salmon may lay directly on the grill, or on an oiled wire screen or sheet of aluminum foil.

Many basting and marinading sauces, as well as seasonings, may be used. The marinade may then also be used as a basting sauce. You may barbecue immediately after applying the seasonings, or allow the salmon to marinate for a few hours, thus letting the flavors penetrate. Some people score the fillets to hasten the soaking-in process.

But a word of caution. If the marinade contains lemon or lime juice, don't let the fish marinate more than an hour or so. Citrus juice tends to "cook" the fish, the method used in preparing saviche from raw fish.

Your first decision, of course, is to decide the seasonings, basting sauce or marinade, you will use on the fish. Following are a few suggestions:

• A popular method is simply to rub the fillets with salt and brown sugar and let stand for a few hours. Then, combine melted butter or margarine with minced garlic cloves or garlic powder, plus some lemon juice to use as a basting sauce.

• Or, simply marinate with barbecue sauce.

• You may use the barbecue sauce just as it comes from the bottle. However, if you feel you must do SOMEthing more add the juice of a lemon, a bit of soy or Worcestershire sauce perhaps, or possibly some melted butter or margarine. The combinations are endless.

Which barbecue sauce to use is up to you. An infinite number of recipes find favor in different parts of the country, and there are those adventurous souls who concoct their own.

• The simplest of all grilling methods—some say the best as the distinctive flavor of salmon is in no way disguised—is just to use melted margarine or butter. Use salt at your discretion.

• Instead of butter or margarine you may simply lay a few strips of bacon over the fish and let the melting fat do the basting for you.

Although smoke adds its own flavor to fish, any of the above suggestions apply even without the use of wood, and you'll still get excellent results.

With Marinade and Without Smoke

Another grilling method for both steaks and fillets, with or without the skin, also features a marinading and basting sauce.

If the salmon is barbecued on aluminum foil it's advisable to curl the edges up to hold the marinade and juices. If the barbecue has no hood a sheet of aluminum laid over the fish helps to reflect the heat down and hold it in.

The lack of smoke, when not laying hardwood on the coals, opens the door to grilling indoors in the oven. The following recipes are marinades which may be used in this type of grilling.

The ingredients are good for two or three pounds of salmon, or four to six average size steaks or fillets, and the directions as related in the foregoing are valid for all of them.

Recognizing the imagination employed by many barbecuing chefs, and thus the varying amounts and ratios of ingredients that may be used, it's difficult to calculate calories and they are not included in these marinading/basting recipes.

GREG JOHNSTON'S CLASSIC MARINADE

(Greg Johnston is the outdoor writer for the Seattle *Post-Intelligencer*, and his recipe for barbecued salmon appeared in John Owen's "Intermediate Eater" column.)

1 or 2 oranges	*1/2 cube butter*
1 garlic clove, minced	*Apple cider vinegar*
Worcestershire sauce	*Chili powder*
Soy sauce	*Tabasco sauce*
Lemon juice	*1 or 2 onions*
	Salt and pepper as desired

(You will note that no precise measurements are given for most ingredients. Culinary adventurers such as John Owen, and free-spirited outdoor writers like Greg Johnston, abhor the strictures of precise recipes. So, as for specific quantities you'll just have to wing it as they are accustomed to doing.)

Rub the fillets with salt and pepper, sprinkle with orange juice, retaining the rinds for later use. Set aside while preparing the sauce.

In a saucepan melt the butter and add garlic, letting it simmer for a moment. Add equal amounts of Worcestershire and soy sauce, lemon juice, vinegar, chili powder and Tabasco to taste.

Sprinkle some sauce on the meat side of the salmon and, when the coals are ready, lay the fillets on the grill, skin side up, for no more than 15 minutes, depending on size.

4. Remove them from the grill and lay them on aluminum foil, skin side down, cover with sauce, sliced onions and the orange rinds, and cook until fish flakes.

❑ 1 ❑ 2 ❑ 3

Directions for the following marinades are all the same unless otherwise noted. Combine the ingredients and marinate the salmon for at least half an hour, then place fish in a greased oven pan and broil or bake as you wish.

If broiled, place the fish four or five inches under heating element for 10 minutes, more or less depending on thickness, or until the fish flakes. After five minutes brush with marinade.

Or, you can bake in a 350-degree oven for 20-25 minutes, again depending on thickness, basting often. After cooking add salt to taste.

CHEF PIERRE'S MARINADE

Salt, ground pepper to taste	*1 TBsp. lemon juice*
3 TBsp. olive oil	*1/2 tsp. lemon juice*
2 TBsp. Dijon-style mustard	*1 TBsp. grated orange rind*
1 TBsp. mustard seed	*1 TBsp. melted butter*
1 tsp. ground cumin seed	*1 TBsp. chopped parsley*

Rub salt and pepper on salmon. Combine remaining ingredients except for butter and parsley. Marinate at room temprerature 30 minutes or more. Remove salmon, add melted butter to marinade, broil salmon, basting often, serve topped with parsley.

❑ 1 ❑ 2 ❑ 3

WHITE WINE MARINADE

1/4 cup salad oil	*1 TBsp. soy sauce*
1 tsp. dill weed	*1/2 cup dry white wine*
1/2 tsp. garlic powder	*1 TBsp. lemon juice*
1/2 tsp. ginger	*Ground black pepper to taste*

❑ 1 ❑ 2 ❑ 3

MARINADE WITH "WRSTRSHR"

1/2 cup ketchup	*1/2 stick melted margarine*
1/4 cup Worcestershire sauce	*1/2 tsp. garlic powder*

❑ 1 ❑ 2 ❑ 3

MARINADE WITH LEMON

1/4 cup lemon juice
1/4 cup salad oil
2 tsp. salt

1/2 tsp. thyme
1 minced garlic clove
Grated rind from one lemon

❏ 1 ❏ 2 ❏ 3

BASIL MARINADE

1/4 cup salad oil
2 TBsp. lemon juice

1/4 tsp. paprika
1/4 tsp. basil

❏ 1 ❏ 2 ❏ 3

MARINADE WITH VERMOUTH

1/2 cup dry vermouth
1/4 cup salad oil
2 TBsp. lemon juice
2 TBsp. finely diced onion

1/4 tsp. each marjoram, pepper
  and thyme
1 minced garlic clove, or 1/2
  tsp. garlic powder

❏ 1 ❏ 2 ❏ 3

'ERB GRILLED SALMON

1 TBsp. parsley flakes
1 tsp. dill weed
1 tsp. lemon pepper

1 TBsp. brown sugar
1/2 tsp. dry mustard
1/4 cup salad oil

❏ 1 ❏ 2 ❏ 3

CURRY MARINADE

1/4 cup salad oil
1/4 tsp. curry powder

2 TBsp. lemon juice

❏ 1 ❏ 2 ❏ 3

ITALIAN MARINADE

1/4 stick melted margarine
1/4 cup Italian dressing

1/4 cup soy sauce
2 TBsp. lemon juice

❏ 1 ❏ 2 ❏ 3

Fresh Chinook salmon from the Washington coast.

❧ 2 ❧

Canned and Flaked Salmon

In a Skillet or Oven Pan

All of the following recipes will use the 8-ounce can, also found in the 7 3/4-ounce size. A thriftier buy is in the 15 1/2-ounce can, and may be divided in half for two different recipes. You may also use salmon left over from some other type of preparation.

As for the various names used—patty, croquette, fritter, cake—all are synonymous as far as these recipes are concerned. Directions are all the same unless otherwise noted. Combine the ingredients, form into patties, coat with crumbs if desired, and fry in oil.

If the mixture is of a consistency that can't be formed into patties, just spoon into the skillet.

Salmon croquettes, fritters, patties, cakes, whatever name you wish to use, are quite often coated with crumbs of some sort. They may be dry bread crumbs, cracker crumbs, or corn flake crumbs. Use whatever you like, or happen to have on hand.

It's also a matter of personal preference whether or not you use a crumb coating at all. It's not at all mandatory, but a coating of crumbs may well enhance the texture and flavor.

QUICKIE CROQUETTES

1 can (8 oz.) salmon	*1 beaten egg*
1/4 cup diced onion	*1/4 tsp. dry mustard*
1 cup soft bread crumbs	*1 TBsp. parsley flakes*
1 TBsp. lemon juice	*Salt and pepper to taste*

❏ 1 ❏ 2 ❏ 3   466 calories

QUICKIE SALMON PATTIES

1 can (8 oz.) salmon
1 TBsp. baking mix
1/2 tsp. lemon pepper

1/4 tsp. salt, or to taste
1 beaten egg
1 cup fresh bread crumbs

❏ 1 ❏ 2 ❏ 3   485 calories

CELERY SALMON PATTIES

1 can (8 oz.) salmon
1 cup fresh bread crumbs
1/2 cup finely diced celery
1/4 tsp. salt, or to taste

1/2 tsp. celery salt
1 TBsp. parsley flakes
1 beaten egg

❏ 1 ❏ 2 ❏ 3   465   calories

SALLY'S SALMON PATTIES

1 can (8 oz.) salmon
1 cup fresh bread crumbs
1/2 cup finely diced celery
1 TBsp. mayonnaise

1 beaten egg
1 TBsp. lemon juice
1 TBsp. flour
1/2 tsp. salt, or to taste

❏ 1 ❏ 2 ❏ 3   570 calories

SALMON CAKES

1 can (8 oz.) salmon
1 cup mashed potatoes
1 TBsp. prepared mustard
1 beaten egg

1/2 cup finely diced onion
1/2 tsp. paprika
1 TBsp. lemon juice
1/4 tsp. salt, or to taste

❏ 1 ❏ 2 ❏ 3   532 calories

SUPER SALMON CAKES

1 can (8 oz.) salmon
1/4 cup finely diced onion
1/4 stick melted margarine
1 cup fresh bread crumbs

1/2 tsp. dry mustard
1 beaten egg
1 TBsp. parsley flakes
1/4 tsp. salt, or to taste

❏ 1 ❏ 2 ❏ 3   646 calories

POTATO/SALMON PATTIES

1 can (8 oz.) salmon
1 cup fresh bread crumbs
1/4 cup finely diced onion
2 TBsp. grated parmesan

1 beaten egg
1/4 tsp. salt, or as needed
Potato Buds or flakes as
  needed

Combine first five ingredients and coat with mashed potato flakes.

❏ 1 ❏ 2 ❏ 3   532 calories

POTATO BUD SALMON

1/4 stick margarine	1 beaten egg
1/2 cup finely diced onion	1/4 tsp. salt, or to taste
1 can (8 oz.) salmon	1/4 tsp. lemon pepper
3 TBsp. fine dry bread crumbs	Potato Buds as needed

In a skillet saute onions in margarine until tender. Combine with next five ingredients, form into patties and coat with Potato Buds.

❏ 1 ❏ 2 ❏ 3   652 calories

WILD WEST CROQUETTES

1 can (8 oz.) salmon	1/4 tsp. salt, or to taste
1 cup fresh bread crumbs	1 beaten egg
1/4 tsp. sage	Crushed corn flake coating

Combine first five ingredients, form into patties and coat with crushed corn flakes.

❏ 1 ❏ 2 ❏ 3   452 calories

FISH PATTIES WITH VEGGIES

1/4 stick margarine	1 TBsp. Worcestershire sauce
1/4 cup diced green pepper	1 beaten egg
1/4 cup finely diced onion	1 can (8 oz.) salmon
1/4 cup finely diced celery	Coating of fine dry bread
1 cup fresh bread crumbs	crumbs (optional)

Saute veggies in margarine until tender. Combine remaining ingredients and coat with crumbs of your choice.

❏ 1 ❏ 2 ❏ 3   656 calories

CAROLINA CROQUETTES

1 can (8 oz.) salmon	1 beaten egg
1/4 cup cornmeal	1 TBsp. mayonnaise
1/2 cup finely diced onion	Salt and pepper to taste
	Corn flake crumbs, if desired

❏ 1 ❏ 2 ❏ 3   692 calories

SALMON/CHEESE NUGGETS

1 can (8 oz.) salmon
1/2 cup mashed potatoes
1/4 cup finely diced onion
1/4 cup finely diced celery

1 TBsp. Worcestershire sauce
Salt and pepper to taste
Cheese cut into 1/2-inch cubes
Crumbs as desired

Combine first six ingredients, then shape into balls around cubed cheese. Roll in crumbs and fry.

❑ 1 ❑ 2 ❑ 3   446 calories, not including cheese and crumbs

CHEESY CROQUETTES

1 can (8 oz.) salmon
1 cup fresh bread crumbs
1/2 cup grated cheese

1 beaten egg
Salt and pepper to taste
Crushed cheese crackers

❑ 1 ❑ 2 ❑ 3   570 calories

BREAKFAST CROQUETTES

1 can (8 oz.) salmon
1/2 cup instant oatmeal
1/4 cup finely diced onion
1/2 cup finely diced celery

1/2 cup finely diced celery
1 beaten egg
Salt and pepper to taste
Corn flake crumbs optional

❑ 1 ❑ 2 ❑ 3   495 calories

BASIC SALMON PATTIES

1 can (8 oz.) salmon
2 eggs, separated
2 TBsp. flour

1/2 tsp. onion salt
1 tsp. parsley flakes
Salt and pepper to taste

Combine fish with beaten egg yokes, flour and seasonings, fold in egg whites and spoon onto a hot, greased skillet.

❑ 1 ❑ 2 ❑ 3   520 calories

SALMON PANCAKES

1 can (8 oz.) salmon
1/2 cup baking mix
1/4 cup diced green onion

1 beaten egg
Salt to taste
Milk as needed

Combine ingredients, adding milk to desired consistency, and spoon onto a hot, greased skillet.

❑ 1 ❑ 2 ❑ 3   631 calories

ONIONY SALMON PATTIES

1/4 stick margarine	*1/4 tsp. salt, or to taste*
1 cup diced onion	*1/4 tsp. onion salt*
1 can (8 oz.) salmon	*1 cup fresh bread crumbs*
	2 beaten eggs

In a skillet saute onion in margarine until tender. Combine with remaining ingredients and form into fritters, or spoon onto a hot, greased skillet.

❏ 1 ❏ 2 ❏ 3   679 calories

SALMON/RICE CROQUETTES

1/4 stick margarine	*1 can (8 oz.) salmon*
1 TBsp. flour	*1 beaten egg*
1/2 cup diced onion	*1/2 cup grated cheese*
1/2 cup milk	*Salt and pepper to taste*
1 cup cooked rice	

In a skillet saute onion in margarine until tender. Add flour and milk, stirring until thickened. Combine with remaining ingredients, form into croquettes and fry in a hot, greased skillet.

❏ 1 ❏ 2 ❏ 3   962 calories

Over Rice, Toast or Muffins

SALMON CURRY

1/4 stick margarine	*1 can (8 oz.) salmon*
1/2 cup diced onion	*1/4 tsp. curry powder*
1 TBsp. flour	*Salt and pepper to taste*
1/2 cup sour cream	

In a skillet saute onion in margarine until tender. Stir in flour then remaining ingredients, stirring until thickened.

❏ 1 ❏ 2 ❏ 3   777 calories

SALMON JAVANESE

1/4 stick margarine	*1 cup cooked rice*
1/2 cup diced onion	*2 TBsp. mayonnaise*
1/4 tsp. garlic powder	*1/4 tsp. curry powder*
1 can (8 oz.) salmon	*Red pepper and salt to taste*

In a skillet saute onion in margarine until tender. Add remaining ingredients, stirring until hot.

❏ 1 ❏ 2 ❏ 3   872 calories

SALMON, EGGS AND CHEESE

1/4 stick margarine	*1 can (8 oz.) salmon*
2 TBsp. flour	*2 hard-boiled eggs, chopped*
1 TBsp. lemon juice	*1/2 cup grated cheese*
4-5 dashes hot pepper sauce	*2 TBsp. diced green onion*
Milk as needed	*Salt and pepper to taste*

In a skillet melt margarine and stir in flour, lemon juice and pepper sauce, stirring in milk until thickened. Add remaining ingredients, stirring until heated.

❏ 1 ❏ 2 ❏ 3   865 calories

SALMON N' SWISS

1/4 stick margarine	*1 TBsp. Worcestershire sauce*
2 TBsp. flour	*1/2 cup cubed Swiss cheese*
1 cup milk, or as needed	*1 can (8 oz.) salmon*

In a saucepan melt margarine, add flour and stir in milk until thickened. Add remaining ingredients, stirring until hot.

❏ 1 ❏ 2 ❏ 3   825 calories

SALMON A LA KING

1/4 stick margarine	*1 can (4 oz.) mushroom pieces,*
1/4 cup diced green pepper	*with liquid*
1/2 cup diced celery	*Milk as needed*
2 TBsp. flour	*1 can (8 oz.) salmon*
	Salt and pepper to taste

In a skillet saute green pepper and celery in margarine until tender. Add mushrooms and flour, slowly stirring in milk until thickened. Add salmon and seasonings, stirring until hot.

❏ 1 ❏ 2 ❏ 3   576 calories

SIMPLE SALMON NEWBERG

1 beaten egg	*1 can (8 oz.) salmon*
2 TBsp. cornstarch	*1/4 stick margarine*
3/4 cup milk, or as needed	*1/4 cup sherry*
	Salt and pepper to taste

In a dish beat egg and cornstarch together. Pour into a saucepan or double boiler and slowly add milk, stirring until thickened. Stir in salmon and margarine, and when the margarine melts add sherry and seasonings.

❏ 1 ❏ 2 ❏ 3   710 calories

FANCY SALMON NEWBERG

1/2 stick margarine
2 TBsp. flour
1 cup milk, or as needed
1 can (8 oz.) salmon

2 eggs, separated
4-5 dashes hot pepper sauce
1/4 cup sherry
Salt and pepper to taste

In a saucepan or double boiler melt margarine and add flour. Stir in milk until thickened, then add flaked salmon.

Separate eggs, combine yokes with salmon mixture, stirring until blended and thickened. Add pepper sauce and sherry.

Beat egg whites stiff and fold into salmon mixture until thoroughly blended. Season to taste.

❏ 1 ❏ 2 ❏ 3   1,050 calories

In a Casserole Dish or Loaf Pan

SALMON CUSTARD

1 TBsp. cornstarch
1/2 cup milk
3 beaten eggs

1 can (8 oz.) salmon
Salt and pepper to taste

In a bowl dissolve cornstarch in milk, add remaining ingredients, turn into a greased casserole dish and bake 30 minutes at 350 degrees.

❏ 1 ❏ 2 ❏ 3   500 calories

SALMON/MUSHROOM QUICHE

1 can cream of mushroom soup
2 beaten eggs

1 can (8 oz.) salmon
2 cups soft bread crumbs

Beat soup and eggs together, then combine all ingredients in a greased casserole dish and bake 30 minutes at 350 degrees.

❏ 1 ❏ 2 ❏ 3   850 calories

MUSHROOM/CHEESE CASSEROLE

1 can (8 oz.) salmon
1 can cream of mushroom soup
1 cup cooked rice

1/2 cup grated cheese
1 cup fresh bread crumbs
12 crushed soda crackers

Combine all but the crackers in a greased casserole dish. Sprinkle crackers over all and bake 30 minutes at 350 degrees.

❏ 1 ❏ 2 ❏ 3   925 calories

SALMON/TOMATO CASSEROLE

1/4 stick margarine
1/2 cup diced onion
1/4 cup diced green pepper
2 TBsp. flour

1 can (8 oz.) tomato sauce
1 can (8 oz.) salmon
12 crushed crackers
Salt and pepper to taste
1 cup fresh bread crumbs

In a skillet saute onion and green pepper in margarine until tender. Add flour and tomato sauce, plus a dab more water to rinse out the can, stirring until thickened.

Combine fish, crackers and seasonings, turn into a greased casserole dish, top with crumbs and bake 30 minutes at 350 degrees.

❑ 1 ❑ 2 ❑ 3   827 calories

QUICKIE SALMON LOAF

1 can (8 oz.) salmon
1/2 cup diced celery
1/2 cup diced onion
2 beaten eggs

12 crushed soda crackers
1/2 cup milk
Salt and pepper to taste

Combine all ingredients in a greased loaf pan and bake 30 minutes at 350 degrees.

❑ 1 ❑ 2 ❑ 3   682 calories

SIMPLE SALMON LOAF

1/4 stick margarine
1/2 cup diced onion
1/2 cup diced celery
2 cups fresh bread crumbs
1 can (8 oz.) salmon

1/2 cup milk
1 TBsp. lemon juice
1 TBsp. parsley flakes
1 beaten egg
Salt and pepper to taste

In a skillet saute onion and celery in margarine until tender. Combine with remaining ingredients, turn into a greased casserole dish and bake 30 minutes at 350 degrees.

❑ 1 ❑ 2 ❑ 3   792 calories

KANSAS KASSEROLE

1/4 stick margarine	1/2 can cream-style corn
1/2 cup diced onion	1/2 cup grated cheese
1 can (8 oz.) salmon	1 beaten egg
1/2 cup milk	Salt and pepper to taste
1 cup fresh bread crumbs	12 crushed soda crackers

In a skillet saute onion in margarine until tender. Combine with other ingredients, except crackers, in a greased casserole dish, cover with crackers and bake 30 minutes at 350 degrees.

❑ 1 ❑ 2 ❑ 3   1,052 calories

PEAS/PASTA CASSEROLE

1 can (8 oz.) salmon	1 TBsp. parsley flakes
1 cup cooked pasta	1 can cream of celery soup
1 cup cooked peas	4 TBsp. grated parmesan cheese
1/4 cup diced green onions	

Combine all but parmesan in a greased casserole dish, sprinkle with cheese and bake 30 minutes at 350 degrees

❑ 1 ❑ 2 ❑ 3   948 calories

PEAS/MUSHROOM CASSEROLE

1 can (8 oz.) salmon	1 cup fresh bread crumbs
1 can cream of mushroom soup	1 tsp. dry mustard
1 cup cooked peas	1 TBsp. Worcestershire sauce
2 TBsp. mayonnaise	12 crushed soda crackers
1 beaten egg	

Combine all but the crackers in a greased casserole dish, sprinkle over with crackers and bake 30 minutes at 350 degrees.

❑ 1 ❑ 2 ❑ 3   1,185 calories

SALMON/CHICKEN CASSEROLE

1 can (8 oz.) salmon	1 can cream of mushroom soup
1 can chicken noodle soup	1 can (4 oz.) evaporated milk
1 can (3 oz.) Chinese noodles	12 crushed soda crackers

Combine all but the crackers in a greased casserole dish, sprinkle over with crackers and bake 30 minutes at 350 degrees.

❑ 1 ❑ 2 ❑ 3   1,261 calories

TOMATO/POTATO CASSEROLE

1 can (8 oz.) salmon
1 cup mashed potatoes
1/2 cup diced onion

1/2 cup diced celery
1 medium tomato, chopped
Salt and pepper to taste

Combine all ingredients in a greased casserole dish and bake 30 minutes at 350 degrees.

❏ 1 ❏ 2 ❏ 3   492 calories

SALMON/PASTA CASSEROLE

1/4 stick margarine
2 TBsp flour
1/2 cup milk, or as needed
1 can (4 oz.) mushroom pieces
  with liquid

1 can (8 oz.) salmon
1/2 cup grated cheddar
Salt and pepper to taste
1 cup cooked pasta
1 cup fresh bread crumbs

In a skillet melt margarine, add flour and mushrooms with liquid, stirring in milk as needed until thickened. Stir in salmon and cheese, adding salt and pepper to taste.

Combine with the pasta in a greased casserole dish, sprinkle over with bread crumbs and bake 30 minutes at 350 degrees.

❏ 1 ❏ 2 ❏ 3   1,023 calories

SALMON/POTATO CHIP CASSEROLE

1/4 stick margarine
1/2 cup diced onion
1/2 cup diced celery
1 cup cooked rice

1 can (8 oz.) salmon
1 can cream of mushroom soup
1 cup crushed potato chips
Salt and pepper to taste

In a skillet saute onion and celery in margarine until tender. Stir in remaining ingredients except potato chips, turn into a greased casserole dish, top with the potato chips and bake 30 minutes at 350 degrees.

❏ 1 ❏ 2 ❏ 3   970 calories

SALMON/POTATO CASSEROLE

1 can (8 oz.) salmon
1 TBsp. Worcestershire sauce
2 TBsp. finely diced onion
1 cup mashed potatoes

1/4 stick margarine
2 TBsp. flour
Salt and pepper to taste
3/4 cup milk, or as needed
1/2 cup grated cheese

Combine salmon, Worcestershire sauce, onion and mashed potatoes in a greased casserole dish.

Make a white sauce by melting margarine in a saucepan and adding flour, stirring in milk until thickened. Season to taste.

Pour over salmon/potato mixture, sprinkle over with cheese and bake 30 minutes at 350 degrees.

❑ 1 ❑ 2 ❑ 3   856 calories

SALMON SOUFFLE

1/4 stick margarine
2 TBsp. flour
1 cup milk, or as needed

1 can (8 oz.) salmon
Salt and pepper to taste
2 eggs, separated

In a skillet or large saucepan melt margarine, add flour and slowly stir in milk as needed to thicken. Stir in the slightly beaten egg yokes and add salt and pepper as desired.

Add the salmon and fold in the stiffly beaten egg whites.

Turn into a greased casserole dish or loaf pan, set in a pan of water and bake 40 minutes at 350 degrees.

NOTE: If you want to fancy up this recipe, add a tablespoon or two of mayonnaise.

❑ 1 ❑ 2 ❑ 3   820 calories

SALMON/ASPARAGUS CASSEROLE

1 can (8 oz.) salmon
1 cup cooked pasta
1/2 cup grated cheddar

1 TBsp. sour cream
1 can cream of asparagus soup
1 cup fresh bread crumbs

Combine all but the bread crumbs in a greased casserole dish, sprinkle over with crumbs and bake 30 minutes at 350 degrees.

❑ 1 ❑ 2 ❑ 3   1,037 calories

FIESTA SALMON (OLE!)

1 can (8 oz.) salmon	1/2 cup cubed Monterey or Swiss
1 cup cooked rice	cheese
1 cup cream-style corn	1 beaten egg
1/4 cup diced green pepper	1/4 tsp. seasoned salt
1/4 cup diced onion	4-5 drops hot pepper sauce

Combine all ingredients in a greased casserole dish and bake 30 minutes at 350 degrees.

❑ 1 ❑ 2 ❑ 3   1,066 calories

CRUNCHY SALMON CASSEROLE

1/4 stick margarine	1/2 tsp. tarragon
1/2 cup diced onion	1 TBsp. parsley flakes
1/2 cup diced celery	1/4 cup milk
1 can (8 oz.) salmon	2 eggs, separated
1/2 cup chopped walnuts	1/2 cup croutons, or 1 slice
Salt and pepper to taste	bread cubed and toasted

In a skillet saute onion and celery in margarine until tender.

Separate eggs and, in a bowl, combine vegetables, salmon, walnuts, seasonings, milk and beaten egg yokes.

Fold in stiffly beaten egg whites, turn into a greased casserole dish, cover with croutons or bread crumbs, set in a pan of water and bake 30 minutes at 350 degrees.

❑ 1 ❑ 2 ❑ 3   972 calories

HOT CHEESY SOUFFLE

2 slices bread, cubed	Dash cayenne pepper
1/2 cup grated cheddar	1/4 cup milk
1/2 tsp. dry mustard	2 eggs, separated
Salt and pepper to taste	1 can (8 oz.) salmon

In a blender combine first six ingredients and blend until smooth. In a bowl combine yokes with contents of blender.

In another bowl beat egg whites stiff and, with salmon, fold into cheese mixture. Turn all into a greased loaf pan, set in a pan of water and bake 30 minutes at 350 degrees.

❑ 1 ❑ 2 ❑ 3   855 calories

FISH AND CHICKEN CASSEROLE

1 can (8 oz.) salmon   *1 can cream of chicken soup*
1 beaten egg   *1 cup bread crumbs*
1 cup cooked rice

Combine first four ingredients in a greased casserole dish, cover with bread crumbs and bake 30 minutes at 350 degrees.

❏ 1 ❏ 2 ❏ 3 860 calories

IMPROBABLE SALMON PIE

1 can (8 oz.) salmon   *1 cup milk*
1/2 cup grated cheddar   *1/2 cup baking mix*
2 TBsp. mayonnaise   *2 eggs*
     1/2 tsp. salt, or to taste

In a bowl combine first three ingredients. Place remaining ingredients in a blender, turn on high for 15 seconds, combine all in a greased oven pan and bake 30 minutes at 400 degrees.

❏ 1 ❏ 2 ❏ 3   1,115 calories

CREAMY FISH CASSEROLE

1 can (8 oz.) salmon   *1/2 tsp. salt*
2 beaten eggs   *1 TBsp. parsley flakes*
1/2 cup half and half or   *1 tsp. onion flakes*
  non-dairy liquid creamer   *1 cup fresh bread crumbs*

Combine all ingredients in a greased oven pan and bake 30 minutes at 350 degrees.

❏ 1 ❏ 2 ❏ 3   599 calories

SALMONARONI

1/2 stick margarine   *1 can (8 oz.) salmon*
2 TBsp. flour   *1 cup cooked macaroni*
1 cup milk, or as needed   *12 crushed soda crackers*
     Salt and pepper to taste

In a skillet melt margarine, add flour and stir in milk until thickened. Combine in a greased casserole dish with salmon and macaroni, season to taste, sprinkle with crushed crackers and bake 30 minutes at 350 degrees.

❏ 1 ❏ 2 ❏ 3   1,110 calories

SALMON AND ONION CASSEROLE

1 can (8 oz.) salmon
1/4 cup diced celery
1 can (4 oz.) mushroom pieces

1 can (3 oz.) French onion
or onion rings
1 can cream of mushroom soup

Combine all ingredients in a greased loaf pan and bake 30 minutes at 350 degrees.

❏ 1 ❏ 2 ❏ 3   638 calories

FISH AND VEGGIE BISCUIT BAKE

1/2 cup diced celery
1/2 cup diced onion
1/2 can (15 oz.) green beans

1 can (8 oz.) salmon
1 can cream of mushroom soup
1/2 cup biscuit mix

Combine veggies, salmon and soup in a greased casserole dish.
Make dough with biscuit mix, lay over mixture and bake 30 minutes at 400 degrees, or until biscuits are brown.

❏ 1 ❏ 2 ❏ 3   647 calories

SALMON ITALIANO

1/4 stick margarine
2 TBsp. flour
1 cup milk
1 can (8 oz.) salmon
1/4 tsp. oregano
1/8 tsp. garlic powder

1 cup cooked pasta
1 can (4 oz.) mushroom pieces
2 TBsp. grated parmesan
Salt and pepper to taste
1 cup fresh bread crumbs

In a skillet melt margarine, add flour and milk, stirring until thickened. Combine all but the crumbs in a greased casserole dish, cover with crumbs and bake 30 minutes at 350 degrees,

❏ 1 ❏ 2 ❏ 3   849 calories

BASIC FISH CASSEROLE

1 can (8 oz.) salmon
2 cups fresh bread crumbs
1 TBsp. parsley
1 TBsp. onion flakes
1 TBsp. mayonnaise

1/2 tsp. celery salt
1/4 cup milk
1 beaten egg
1 TBsp. lemon juice
Salt and pepper to taste

In a bowl combine all ingredients. Turn into a greased casserole dish and bake 30 minutes at 350 degrees.

❏ 1 ❏ 2 ❏ 3   640 calories

SPEEDY SALMON LOAF

1 can (8 oz.) salmon	*1 TBsp. lemon juice*
1 cup fresh bread crumbs	*1 TBsp. parsley flakes*
1/2 cup finely diced onion	*1/2 tsp. seafood seasoning*
1/2 cup finely diced celery	*2 beaten eggs*
1/2 cup milk	*Salt and pepper to taste*

In a bowl combine all ingredients. Turn into a greased casserole dish and bake 30 minutes at 350 degrees.

❑ 1 ❑ 2 ❑ 3   632 calories

SPICY RICE AND CHEESE CASSEROLE

1 can (8 oz.) salmon	*1/4 tsp. chili powder*
1 can (8 oz.) tomato sauce	*1/8 tsp. cayenne*
1 cup cooked rice	*Salt to taste*
1/2 cup grated cheddar	*Dash of garlic powder*

In a bowl combine all ingredients. Turn into a greased casserole dish and bake 30 minutes at 350 degrees.

❑ 1 ❑ 2 ❑ 3   975 calories

TANGY AU GRATIN CASSEROLE

1/4 stick margarine	*Salt and pepper to taste*
2 TBsp. flour	*1 can (8 oz.) salmon*
1/4 tsp. dry mustard	*1 cup grated cheese*
1 cup milk, or as needed	*1 cup fresh bread crumbs*

In a skillet add flour and mustard to melted margarine, stirring in milk until thickened. Add seasonings to taste. Combine with remaining ingredients, turn into a greased casserole dish and bake 30 minutes at 350 degrees.

❑ 1 ❑ 2 ❑ 3   1,055 calories

SALMON/CHEESE PIE

1/4 stick margarine	*1 cup grated cheddar*
1/2 cup diced onion	*1 cup cooked peas*
2 TBsp. flour	*1 can (8 oz.) salmon*
1 cup milk	*1/2 cup biscuit mix, or*
1 TBsp. Worcestershire sauce	*as needed*

In a skillet saute onion in margarine until tender. Add flour, slowly stirring in milk until thickened. Add next four ingredients and turn into a greased casserole dish.

Top with biscuit mix dough and bake 40 minutes at 350 degrees, or until biscuits are brown.

❑ 1 ❑ 2 ❑ 3   1,312 calories

SALMON/SPLIT PEA PIE

1/4 stick margarine	*1 can cond. split pea soup*
1/2 cup diced onion	*1/2 cup milk*
1/2 cup diced celery	*1 can (8 oz.) salmon*
1/2 cup diced potato	*1/2 cup biscuit mix*

In a skillet saute veggies in margarine until tender. Combine in a greased casserole dish with the soup, milk and salmon.

Top with biscuit mix dough and bake 40 minutes at 350 degrees, or until biscuits are brown.

❏ 1 ❏ 2 ❏ 3   1,127 calories

POTATO/ONION LOAF

1/4 stick margarine	*1 cup mashed potatoes*
1 cup diced onion	*1 TBsp. parsley flakes*
1 can (8 oz.) salmon	*1/4 cup milk*
2 eggs, separated	*Salt and pepper to taste*

In a skillet saute onion in margarine until tender.

Separate eggs, combine yokes with remaining ingredients. Fold in whites beaten stiff, turn into a greased casserole dish, place in a pan of water and bake 40 minutes at 350 degrees.

❏ 1 ❏ 2 ❏ 3   864 calories

LOAF WITH PICKLE RELISH

1 can (8 oz.) salmon	*1/4 cup milk*
2 cups soft bread crumbs	*2 beaten eggs*
2 TBsp. pickle relish	*Salt and pepper to taste*

In a bowl combine all ingredients. Turn into a greased casserole dish and bake 30 minutes at 350 degrees.

❏ 1 ❏ 2 ❏ 3   975 calories

SALMON/GREEN BEAN LOAF

1/4 stick margarine	*1/2 cup grated cheddar*
2 TBsp. flour	*1 can (16 oz.) cut green beans*
1 cup milk, or as needed	*1 can (8 oz.) salmon*
Salt and pepper to taste	*1 cup fresh bread crumbs*

In a large saucepan make a white sauce with flour and milk. Combine with seasonings, cheese, beans and salmon in a greased casserole dish, top with bread crumbs and bake 30 minutes at 350 degrees. Use asparagus tips or broccoli instead of green beans if you wish.

❏ 1 ❏ 2 ❏ 3   850 calories

SALMON/BROCCOLI LOAF

1 pkg. (10 oz.) frozen
  chopped broccoli
1/2 cup diced onion
1/4 stick margarine
1 can cream of mushroom soup

1 can (4 oz.) mushroom pieces
1 can (8 oz.) salmon
2 TBsp. parmesan cheese
2 TBsp. lemon juice

Cook broccoli and drain. In a skillet saute onion in margarine. Combine all ingredients in a greased casserole dish and bake 30 minutes at 350 degrees.

❑ 1 ❑ 2 ❑ 3   853 calories

SALMON/HARD-BOILED EGG LOAF

1/4 stick margarine
2 TBsp. flour
1 cup milk, or as needed
1 can (8 oz.) salmon

2 cups fresh bread crumbs
1/2 tsp. onion powder
2 hard-boiled eggs, chopped
Salt and pepper to taste

In a skillet add flour to margarine and stir in milk until thickened. Combine with remaining ingredients, turn into a greased casserole dish and bake 30 minutes at 350 degrees.

❑ 1 ❑ 2 ❑ 3   950 calories

Simple Salmon Sandwiches

Ingredients in the following recipes are to be combined and spread on bread, buttered or otherwise, with lettuce and tomatoes as desired. Calorie counts include only the ingredients listed.

Recipes call for two tablespoons of mayonnaise, but this is not chiseled in stone due to certain variables. One is the amount of mayonnaise that can be placed on a tablespoon, from level to heaping. Another is that some mayonnaise, such as lo-cal, may have less consistency than regular. Also, dryness of the salmon can be a factor.

A suggestion would be to combine all but the mayonnaise, then add a little at a time until reaching the desired consistency.

NUTTY SALMON SANDWICH

1 can (8 oz.) salmon
1/2 cup finely diced celery

1/4 cup chopped walnuts
2 TBsp. mayonnaise

❑ 1 ❑ 2 ❑ 3   695 calories

SALMON AND SWEET PICKLE

1 can (8 oz.) salmon
2 TBsp. sweet pickle relish
2 TBsp. finely diced onion

2 TBsp. finely diced celery
2 TBsp. mayonnaise
Salt and pepper to taste

❑ 1 ❑ 2 ❑ 3   505 calories

SALMON SANDWICH WITH DILL

1 can (8 oz.) salmon
2 TBsp. finely diced celery
2 TBsp. mayonnaise

2 TBsp. lemon juice
1/4 tsp. dill weed
Salt and pepper to taste

❑ 1 ❑ 2 ❑ 3   490 calories

SMOKY SALMON SANDWICH

1 can (8 oz.) salmon
2 TBsp. mayonnaise

1/4 cup diced dill pickle
Smoke-flavored salt to taste

❑ 1 ❑ 2 ❑ 3   490 calories

SALMON SANDWICH WITH MUSTARD

1 can (8 oz.) salmon
2 TBsp. mayonnaise

2 TBsp. diced dill pickle
1 TBsp. prepared mustard

❑ 1 ❑ 2 ❑ 3   495 calories

SALMON SANDWICH WITH "WRSTRSHR"

1 can (8 oz.) salmon
2 TBsp. mayonnaise

2 TBsp. finely diced onion
1 TBsp. Worcestershire sauce

❑ 1 ❑ 2 ❑ 3   500 calories

CHEESY SALMON SANDWICH

1 can (8 oz.) salmon
1 hard-boiled egg, chopped
2 TBsp. mayonnaise
1 TBsp. lemon juice

1/4 tsp. dill weed
1/4 cup finely diced celery
1/2 cup grated cheddar
1 tsp. prepared mustard

❑ 1 ❑ 2 ❑ 3   745 calories

THREE-WAY CHEESY SANDWICH

1 can (8 oz.) salmon
1/2 cup grated cheese
2 TBsp. finely diced onion

1 TBsp. Worcestershire sauce
4-5 drops hot pepper sauce
1/4 stick melted margarine

Option 1. Combine all ingredients, adding melted margarine last, and use as a regular sandwich filler.

Option 2. Spread on bread, place on an oven pan and toast under the broiling element until brown.

Option 3. Spread on bread, butter lightly on both sides and toast in a skillet.

❏ 1 ❏ 2 ❏ 3   665 calories

SWISS SANDWICH WITH "WSRSTRSHR"

1 can (8 oz.) salmon
2 TBsp. mayonnaise

2 TBsp. finely diced onion
1 TBsp. Worcestershire sauce

❏ 1 ❏ 2 ❏ 3   500 calories

A common sight on docks these days.

꙰ 3 ꙰

Bottomfish Fillets

These recipes may be used with most any white-meated fish, whether or not they are listed under the catch-all designation of bottomfish, or groundfish. This is not to say that all white-meated fish are the same. Some are more firm than others, some flakier, and the oil content and flavor may vary.

Nevertheless, be it one of the many rockfish species, other marine fish such as lingcod, true cod and black cod, plus the many white-meated freshwater species, can all be used in these recipes.

There are, however, separate chapters on halibut, smelt and shad, as well as the walleyed pike, which devotees claim to be the choice table fare of all the freshwater species.

The dogfish is also an edible species, but doesn't often find its way to the table due to the care that must be taken to remove the uric acid found in the flesh. Fillets may be soaked for a few hours in a light solution of lemon juice or vinegar, and used in any of the following recipes. It's quite bland, however, and needs pepping up to be palatable.

Halibut may also be used in any of this chapter's recipes. However, this highly-regarded rival of salmon, with its firm, flaky and flavorful flesh, rightfully deserves to be dealt with separately.

In the Skillet

FILLETS IN BATTER

This is a simple cooking method which lends itself to quick preparation for anywhere from a single person to a crowd. Also, the quantity of batter can be tailored to the amount of fish. Or if there is an excess of batter it can be saved for later use.

Directions for the following recipes are the same. Combine all ingredients and fry hot and fast in a greased skillet, or deep-fry in hot oil. Calorie counts do not include the fish or the oil as varying amounts of both may be used. The recipes are adequate for a pound or more of fillets.

A baking mix containing a leavener is called for in all recipes, although an all-purpose flour may also be used.

BASIC BATTER

1/2 cup baking mix   *1/2 cup milk, or as needed*
1 beaten egg   *Salt and pepper to taste*

❑ 1 ❑ 2 ❑ 3   460 calories

PUFF BATTER

1/2 cup baking mix   *1 beaten egg*
1 TBsp. cornstarch   *Salt and pepper to taste*
                                  Cold water as needed

❑ 1 ❑ 2 ❑ 3   310 calories

MY LITTLE MARGIE

1/2 cup baking mix   *1 beaten egg*
1/2 tsp. marjoram   *1/4 cup milk, or as needed*
                                  Salt and pepper to taste

❑ 1 ❑ 2 ❑ 3   310 calories

CORNMEAL BATTER

1/4 cup cornmeal   *1 beaten egg*
1/4 cup baking mix   *1/4 cup milk, or as needed*
                                  Salt and pepper to taste

❑ 1 ❑ 2 ❑ 3   450 calories

OAHU BATTER

1/2 cup crushed pineapple   *2 TBsp. baking mix*
1 beaten egg   *1/4 tsp. salt*
                                  1/2 cup milk

❑ 1 ❑ 2 ❑ 3   576 calories

BEER BATTER

1/2 cup baking mix   1 tsp. paprika
1/2 cup beer, or as needed   Salt to taste

❏ 1 ❏ 2 ❏ 3   490 calories

CRISPY BATTER

1/2 cup baking mix   1 TBsp. salad oil
1 tsp. sugar   Salt to taste
     Water as needed

❏ 1 ❏ 2 ❏ 3   398 calories

Coated Fillets

Coated fillets are dipped in a liquid such as milk or beaten egg, then coated with a mix of various ingredients. Principal purpose of the liquid is to aid the coating mix in adhering to the fish. As with a batter-coated fillet, they may be either fried in a skillet or deep-fried. In deep-frying it's customary to cut the fillets into bite-sized cubes.

They may also be baked in an oven pan. A baking time of 20 minutes at 350 degrees would be adequate in most cases.

The following recipes make enough coating mix for a pound of fish or more. Calorie counts include only ingredients listed.

NOTE: Directions are the same for all recipes unless otherwise indicated. Sift flour over the fillets, dip in milk or egg, according to the recipe, before coating with remaining ingredients.

POTATO BUD FILLETS

2 TBsp. flour, or as needed   1/2 cup Potato Buds, or as
1/4 cup milk, or as needed   needed
1 beaten egg   Salt and pepper to taste

❏ 1 ❏ 2 ❏ 3   290 calories

CRISPY FRIED FILLETS

2 TBsp. flour, or as needed   1/4 cup baking mix
1/4 cup milk   1 tsp. paprika
1/4 cup cornmeal   Salt and pepper to taste

❏ 1 ❏ 2 ❏ 3   340 calories

WITH LEMON PEPPER SEASONING

2 TBsp. flour, or as needed   1 tsp. lemon pepper seasoning
1 beaten egg   Salt and pepper to taste
1/2 cup cornmeal

❑ 1 ❑ 2 ❑ 3   400 calories

BUTTERMILK FILLETS

2 TBsp. flour   1/2 cup baking mix
Buttermilk as needed   Salt and pepper to taste

❑ 1 ❑ 2 ❑ 3   280 calories

ZIPPY FILLETS

2 TBsp. flour   1/4 tsp. cayenne pepper
Buttermilk as needed   1/4 tsp. black pepper
1/2 cup cornmeal   1/2 tsp. salt

❑ 1 ❑ 2 ❑ 3   330 calories

RITZY FILLETS

2 TBsp. flour   1/2 tsp. garlic powder
1 beaten egg   1/2 tsp. onion powder
                               1/2 cup crushed Ritz crackers

❑ 1 ❑ 2 ❑ 3   330 calories

COD CALIENTE

2 TBsp. flour   1/2 tsp. chili powder
1 beaten egg   1/8 tsp. cayenne pepper
1/4 cup baking mix   1/2 tsp. oregano
1/4 cup cornmeal   1/2 tsp. salt

❑ 1 ❑ 2 ❑ 3   380 calories

PARMESAN FILLETS

1/4 cup olive oil
1/4 cup soy sauce
4-5 dashes hot pepper sauce

1/4 cup fine dry bread crumbs,
  or as needed
2 TBsp. parmesan cheese

Marinate fillets in olive oil, soy sauce and hot pepper sauce for an hour or more, then coat with combined bread crumbs and parmesan cheese.

NOTE: An option would be, after marinating, to sprinkle the fillets with both garlic and onion powder, plus table salt. Bake 20 minutes at 350 degrees.

❑ 1 ❑ 2 ❑ 3   679 calories

Keep the Skillet Hot

VEGGIE FISH DISH

1/4 stick margarine
1/2 cup diced onion
1/2 cup diced celery
1/2 cup chopped tomatoes

1/2 cup sliced mushrooms, or
1 can (4 oz.) pieces & stems
1/2 lb. fillets
Salt and pepper to taste

In a skillet saute veggies in margarine until tender. Add seasonings and fillets, cover and simmer 10-15 minutes, or until fish flakes.

❑ 1 ❑ 2 ❑ 3   523 calories

FANCY VEGGIE FISH DISH

1/4 stick margarine
1/2 cup diced onion
1/2 cup diced celery
1/2 cup diced green pepper

1 can (4 oz.) mushroom pieces
1 can cream of tomato soup
1 cup fresh bread crumbs
1/2 lb. fillets

In a skillet saute onion, celery and green pepper in margarine until tender. Stir in remaining ingredients, cover and simmer 10-15 minutes or until fish flakes.

❑ 1 ❑ 2 ❑ 3   797 calories

LO-CAL COD N' VEGGIES

1/2 cup diced potatoes	1 cup chicken bouillon
1/2 cup diced carrots	1/2 lb. fillets
1/2 cup diced celery	2 TBsp. chives

In a skillet simmer veggies in bouillon until tender. Add fish, sprinkle with chives, cover and simmer until fish flakes. Remove with a slotted spatula and discard bouillon.

❑ 1 ❑ 2 ❑ 3   350 calories

SPICY FILLETS

1 beaten egg	2 TBsp. lemon juice
1/4 chili powder	1/4 tsp. garlic powder
1/2 tsp. turmeric	1/2 lb. fillets
1 tsp. salt	1/2 cup fine dry bread crumbs

Combine first six ingredients and use this to marinate the fillets for an hour or more. Coat with bread crumbs and fry.

❑ 1 ❑ 2 ❑ 3   450 calories

SPICY TOMATO N' COD

1/4 stick margarine	1/4 tsp. thyme
1 clove garlic, diced	1/4 tsp. ground bay leaf
1/2 cup diced onion	1/2 tsp. salt, or to taste
1/2 cup diced green pepper	1/8 tsp. cayenne pepper
1 cup chopped tomato	1/2 lb. fillets

In a skillet saute garlic, onion and green pepper in margarine until tender. Add tomatoes, seasonings and fillets, cover and simmer 10-15 minutes or until fish flakes.

❑ 1 ❑ 2 ❑ 3   514 calories

WINE N' CHILI FISH DISH

1/4 stick margarine	1/4 cup dry white wine
1/2 cup diced onion	2 TBsp. chili sauce
1 can (4 oz.) mushroom pieces	1/2 lb. fillets
1 cup chopped tomato	Salt and pepper to taste

Saute onion in margarine until tender. Stir in remaining ingredients, cover and simmer 10-15 minutes or until fish flakes.

❑ 1 ❑ 2 ❑ 3   550 calories

WITH CHICKEN N' CHEESE

1/4 stick margarine
1 TBsp. flour
2 beaten eggs

1 cup chicken bouillon
1/2 lb. fillets
1/2 cup grated cheese

In a skillet stir flour into margarine, add eggs and bouillon, stirring until blended. Add fillets, sprinkle with cheese, cover and simmer 10-15 minutes or until fish flakes.

❏ 1 ❏ 2 ❏ 3   850 calories

HOT CREAMY COD

1/4 stick margarine
1/2 cup diced onion
1 TBsp. cornstarch
1 cup milk, half and half or
    non-dairy liquid creamer

1 TBsp. lemon juice
1/2 tsp. thyme
1/8 tsp. white pepper
1/2 tsp. salt, or to taste
1/2 lb. fillets

In a skillet saute onion in margarine until tender.
Dissolve cornstarch in liquid, combine with remaining ingredients—except fillets—in skillet, stirring until thickened. Add fillets, cover and cook until fish flakes.

❏ 1 ❏ 2 ❏ 3   697 calories

COD N' CURRY

1/4 stick margarine
1 cup diced celery
1 cup diced onion

1/4 tsp. curry powder
1/2 tsp. salt, or to taste
1/2 lb. fillets

In a skillet saute celery and onion in margarine until tender. Stir in seasonings and add fillets. Cover and cook 10-15 minutes or until fish flakes.

❏ 1 ❏ 2 ❏ 3   484 calories

TOMATO/ZUCCHINI COD

1/4 stick margarine
1 cup sliced zucchini
1 can cream of mushroom soup

2 TBsp. sour cream
1 cup chopped tomato
1/2 lb. fillets

In a skillet saute sliced, unpeeled zucchini in margarine until tender. Add soup, sour cream and tomato, stirring until heated. Add fish and simmer 10-15 minutes or until fish flakes.

❏ 1 ❏ 2 ❏ 3   830 calories

CARLA'S COD

1/4 stick margarine	1 can (4 oz.) chopped ripe
1/2 cup diced onion	olives, or 1/2 cup
1/2 cup green pepper	1/4 cup sherry
1 can (4 oz.) mushroom pieces	1/2 lb. fillets
1 cup chopped tomato	Salt and pepper to taste

In a skillet saute onion and green pepper in margarine until tender. Add remaining ingredients, season to taste, cover and simmer 10-15 minutes or until fish flakes.

❏ 1 ❏ 2 ❏ 3   692 calories

LYNN CHAMBERLIN'S ROCKFISH DELIGHT

1 TBsp. sherry wine	1/4 stick margarine
1 TBsp. lemon juice	1/8 tsp. garlic powder
1 TBsp. Worcestershire sauce	1/2 tsp. sesame seed
1 tsp. soy sauce	1/2 tsp. dill weed
1 Tbsp. olive oil	1/2 lb. fillets, cubed

Combine all ingredients but fillets in a skillet, stirring until heated. Add cubed fillets, stirring until fish flakes.

❏ 1 ❏ 2 ❏ 3   535 calories

FILLETS WITH A TANG

1/4 stick margarine	1 TBsp. Worcestershire sauce
1/2 cup diced onion	1 TBsp. vinegar
1/2 cup diced celery	Salt and pepper to taste
1/2 cup diced green pepper	1/2 cup water
2 TBsp. ketchup	1 TBsp. cornstarch
1 TBsp. prepared mustard	1/2 lb. fillets

In a skillet saute veggies in margarine until tender. Stir in ketchup, mustard, Worcestershire sauce, vinegar and seasonings. Add cornstarch dissolved in water, stirring until thickened. Add fillets, cover and simmer 10-15 minutes or until fish flakes.

❏ 1 ❏ 2 ❏ 3   494 calories

ONION/CUSTARD COD

1/4 stick margarine
1/2 cup diced onion
2 TBsp. cornstarch
1 cup chicken bouillon

1 TBsp. ketchup
1/2 tsp. dry mustard
1/2 lb. fillets
Salt and pepper to taste

In a skillet saute onion in margarine until tender. Dissolve cornstarch in bouillon and add to skillet with ketchup and mustard, stirring until it starts to thicken. Add fillets, cover and simmer 10-15 minutes or until fish flakes.

❏ 1 ❏ 2 ❏ 3   457 calories

WITH TOMATO SAUCE

1/4 stick margarine
1/2 cup diced onion
1/2 cup diced celery
1/4 tsp. garlic powder

1 can (8 oz.) tomato sauce
1 TBsp. Worcestershire sauce
Salt and pepper to taste
1/2 lb. fillets

In a skillet saute onion in margarine until tender. Add remaining ingredients, cover and simmer 10-15 minutes or until fish flakes.

❏ 1 ❏ 2 ❏ 3   772 calories

FILLETS AND SPAGHETTI

1/4 stick margarine
1/2 cup diced onion
1 clove garlic, diced
1 can (8 oz.) tomato sauce
1 can (15 oz.) crushed
   tomatoes
1 can (4 oz.) mushroom pieces

1/2 tsp. rosemary
1/2 tsp. basil
1/2 tsp. salt, or to taste
2 TBsp. cornstarch
1/2 lb. fillets, cubed
Cooked spaghetti as desired
Grated parmesan as desired

In a deep skillet or saucepan saute onion and garlic in margarine until tender. Add tomato sauce, tomatoes and seasonings. Add cornstarch, dissolved in a bit of water, stirring until blended and starts to thicken. Add cubed fillets, cover and simmer 10-15 minutes or until fish flakes, spoon over spaghetti and top with parmesan cheese.

❏ 1 ❏ 2 ❏ 3   870 calories, not including pasta and cheese

FILLETS ITALIANO

1 cup soft bread crumbs　　　　*1/2 tsp. salt, or to taste*
3 TBsp. grated parmesan　　　　*1 beaten egg*
1 TBsp. parsley flakes　　　　*1/2 lb. fillets*
1/2 tsp. garlic powder　　　　*Olive oil as needed*

In a blender combine bread crumbs, parmesan, garlic powder and salt. Dip fillets in beaten egg, dredge in blended crumb mixture and fry in olive oil until golden brown.

❏ 1 ❏ 2 ❏ 3　　580 calories

FILLETS ITALIANO FORTISSIMO

Follow directions for the above, then pour tomato sauce over fillets, cover and simmer until sauce is hot, place a slice of mozzarella on each fillet and simmer until cheese melts.

❏ 1 ❏ 2 ❏ 3　　1,060 calories

FILLETS ITALIANO MUCHO FORTISSIMO

Follow directions for the above, but to the tomato sauce add sliced olives, mushroom pieces, oregano and garlic powder in amounts desired. Cover and simmer until sauce is hot, then place a slice of mozzarella on each fillet and simmer until cheese melts.

❏ 1 ❏ 2 ❏ 3　　1,060 calories, except olives and mushrooms

In An Oven Pan

BAKED WITH A MAYONNAISE TOPPING

A simple method of baking a fillet, for one person or many, is topping it with an equal amount of sour cream or plain yogurt, plus horseradish. The horseradish may be mild or hot, depending on your preference.

Another suggestion is to mix the mayonnaise with some type of dry wine, according to your preference or what you have on hand.

Sprinkle salt and pepper on the fillets as you wish, cover with the mayonnaise mixture and bake in a greased oven pan for 20-25 minutes at 350 degrees.

An additional touch would be to sprinkle lemon juice over the fillets before covering with the mayonnaise mixture, then sprinkling with paprika.

If you're in a REAL big hurry, sprinkle on some lemon pepper seasoning and bake 15 minutes at 400 degrees.

WITH SALAD DRESSING

Another simple method of preparing a fillet of almost any type is to cut it into bite-sized portions, marinate them for a few hours in the salad dressing of your choice, place them in a greased oven pan and bake for 20-25 minutes at 350 degrees.

Instead of baking you may may also microwave them, covered, for four minutes, or thereabouts.

DAYLE'S FISH BROIL ALYESKA

2 TBsp. mayonnaise
2 TBsp. sour cream
2 TBsp. chopped green onion

1 TBsp. lemon juice
1 TBsp. Worcestershire sauce
1/2 lb. fillets
3 TBsp. grated parmesan

Combine first five ingredients, cover fillets, top with parmesan, place on a greased oven pan and broil 6 to 8 minutes, or until fish flakes. Or, bake 20-25 minutes at 350 degrees.

❏ 1 ❏ 2 ❏ 3   316 calories

WITH YOGURT AND CHEESE

1/2 lb. fillets
1/4 cup diced green onion
1/4 cup plain yogurt

1/2 tsp. salt, or to taste
Dash of dill
2 TBsp. grated parmesan

Lay fillets in a greased oven pan. Cover with remaining ingredients, except cheese. Bake 15-20 minutes at 350 degrees, sprinkle over with parmesan and broil until cheese starts turning brown.

❏ 1 ❏ 2 ❏ 3   436 calories

QUICKIE FISH BAKE

1/2 lb. fillets
Flour as needed
1 beaten egg
1/2 cup crushed crackers

1/2 tsp. lemon pepper
1 tsp. seafood seasoning
1 tsp. parsley flakes
1/4 stick melted margarine

Flour fillets, dip in beaten egg, dredge in cracker crumbs in which seasonings have been combined, arrange in greased oven pan, drizzle with margarine and bake 20-25 minutes at 350 degrees.

❏ 1 ❏ 2 ❏ 3   620 calories

CHIPS N' FILLET BAKE

1/2 lb. fillets
1/4 cup Italian dressing

1/2 cup crushed potato chips
2 TBsp. grated parmesan

Dip fillets in Italian dressing, dredge in combined potato chips and parmesan, arrange in a greased oven pan and bake 20-25 minutes at 350 degrees.

❏ 1 ❏ 2 ❏ 3   686 calories

WITH KETCHUP AND WINE

1/2 lb. fillets
Salt and pepper to taste
1/2 cup diced green onion

4 TBsp. ketchup
2 TBsp. salad oil
1/2 cup dry white wine

Arrange seasoned fish in a greased oven pan. Combine remaining ingredients, pour over the fish and bake 20-25 minutes at 350 degrees.

❏ 1 ❏ 2 ❏ 3   552 calories

WITH WORCESTERSHIRE SAUCE

1/2 lb. fillets
1/2 tsp. onion powder

3 TBsp. salad oil
3 TBsp. Worcestershire sauce

Arrange seasoned fillets in a greased oven pan. Combine oil and Worcestershire sauce, pour over fillets and bake 20-25 minutes at 350 degrees. After cooking, pour the remaining sauce over the fillets.

❏ 1 ❏ 2 ❏ 3   600 calories

TOMATO/FISH BAKE

1/2 lb. fillets
1 can (16 oz.) crushed
* tomatoes*

2 TBsp. parsley flakes
2 TBsp. onion flakes
1/4 stick melted margarine

Arrange fillets in a greased oven pan, cover with remaining ingredients and bake 20-25 minutes at 350 degrees.

❏ 1 ❏ 2 ❏ 3   440 calories

ASPARAGUS FISH BAKE

1/2 lb. fillets
1/4 cup diced green onion
1 can cream of asparagus soup

1/4 cup dry white wine
4 TBsp. grated parmesan,
   or as desired

Arrange fillets in a greased oven pan. Sprinkle over with green onion, pour combined soup and wine over all, sprinkle with parmesan cheese and bake 20-25 minutes at 350 degrees.

❑ 1 ❑ 2 ❑ 3   680 calories

KELLI'S KOD KURRY

1/2 lb. fillets
1 cup cooked rice

1/8 tsp. curry powder
1/4 stick melted margarine
Salt to taste

Arrange fillets in a greased oven pan, pour over with remaining ingredients and bake 20-25 minutes at 350 degrees.

❑ 1 ❑ 2 ❑ 3   600 calories

GOLDEN NUGGETS

Cut the fillets into bite-sized cubes, coat with oil, roll in a mixture of half fine, dry bread crumbs and grated parmesan, place in a greased oven pan and bake 15 minutes at 400 degrees.

❑ 1 ❑ 2 ❑ 3

TOMATO/CHEESE FISH BAKE

1/2 lb. fillets
1/4 cup diced green onion

1 sliced tomato
1 cup grated cheese

Arrange fillets in a greased oven pan, sprinkle over with green onion, top with tomato slices, cover with grated cheese and bake 20-25 minutes at 350 degrees.

❑ 1 ❑ 2 ❑ 3   621 calories

FISH AND MUSHROOM BAKE

1/2 lb. fillets
1/2 cup diced green onion
1 cup fresh bread crumbs

1/4 stick melted margarine
1 can cream of mushroom soup

Arrange fillets in a greased oven pan, pour over with remaining ingredients and bake 20-25 minutes at 350 degrees.

❑ 1 ❑ 2 ❑ 3   746 calories

TOMATO SAUCE AND CHEESE BAKE

1/2 lb. fillets
2 TBsp. onion flakes

1 can (8 oz.) tomato sauce
1 cup grated cheese

Arrange fillets in a greased oven pan, cover with combined onion flakes and tomato sauce, sprinkle over with grated cheese and bake 20-25 minutes at 350 degrees.

❑ 1 ❑ 2 ❑ 3   730 calories

BUD'S BAKED FISH

1 cup water
1 TBsp. onion flakes
2 TBsp. lemon juice
1/4 stick margarine

2 TBsp. flour
Salt and pepper to taste
1/2 lb. fillets
1 cup grated cheese

In a saucepan combine onion flakes and lemon juice with the water and bring to a boil. Melt margarine in a double boiler, add the flour and stir in the liquid from the saucepan until it starts to thicken, seasoning to taste.

Arrange fillets in a greased oven, cover with the sauce, sprinkle over with grated cheese and bake 20-25 minutes at 350 degrees.

❑ 1 ❑ 2 ❑ 3   800 calories

FILLETS AMANDINE

1/2 lb. fillets
2 TBsp. flour
1 TBsp. paprika
1/2 tsp. salt, pepper to taste

1/4 stick melted margarine
1 TBsp. lemon juice
4-5 dashes hot pepper sauce
1/4 cup slivered almonds

Coat fillets with combined flour and seasonings and arrange in a greased oven pan. Combine margarine, lemon juice and pepper sauce, pour over fillets, sprinkle with almonds and bake 20-25 minutes at 350 degrees.

❑ 1 ❑ 2 ❑ 3   610 calories

FILLETS CALIFORNIA

1/2 lb. fillets
Salt and pepper to taste
1/4 stick margarine
1/2 cup diced celery
1/2 cup diced onion

1/4 cup chopped walnuts
1 cup soft bread crumbs
1 tsp. grated orange rind
*   (optional but recommended)*
1/4 cup orange juice

Season fillets as desired and place in a greased oven pan.

In a skillet saute celery and onion in margarine until tender. Add remaining ingredients, spread over fillets and bake 20-25 minutes at 350 degrees.

❏ 1 ❏ 2 ❏ 3   742 calories

CRISPY FILLETS

1/2 lb. fillets
Salt to taste
3 TBsp. mayonnaise
1 cup crushed potato chips

2 TBsp. grated parmesan
1 TBsp. onion flakes
*   (or as desired)*

Season fillets, keeping in mind the salt that may be in the potato chips, and arrange in a greased oven pan. Combine mayonnaise, parmesan and onion flakes, spread over fillets, sprinkle on the potato chips and bake 20-25 minutes at 350 degrees.

❏ 1 ❏ 2 ❏ 3   691 calories

Grilled—In the Oven or Over the Coals

The scene was never recorded, of course, but in all likelihood the first method of fish cookery employed by the primitive ancestors of man was over live coals. And that method is still being used today. If there is a difference, modern day grilling, or broiling, can also be done in the kitchen using the upper heating heating element in the oven.

Fillets are usually grilled with the skin still attached, thus holding the meat together as it cooks. Skinless fillets, as well as steaks, may be grilled using a wire basket with a moveable top that holds the fish firmly. Such a basket is especially recommended for cooking over coals as the fish can be easily turned to cook and to baste both sides with a basting sauce.

When grilling in the oven the distance from the fish to the heating element should be around four inches, more or less, depending on thickness of the fillet. In any event, the fish is done when it flakes easily with a fork.

You can, if you wish, bake the fish instead of grilling. By rule of thumb, 15 to 20 minutes at 350 degrees should be adequate. DON'T

OVERCOOK. Too much cooking causes the fish to become dry and less palatable.

Fish may be grilled using just the basic seasonings, salt and pepper. However, marinades such as the following impart an entirely different character. Immerse the fish in the marinade for at least a half hour, or for many hours. If you wish you may spoon some of the leftover marinade over the fish after cooking.

STAN JONES MARINADE

1/2 cup salad oil	1/2 tsp. rosemary
1/4 cup lemon juice	1/4 tsp. ground bay leaves
1 tsp. salt	1/4 cup diced green onion
2 TBsp. parsley flakes	1/4 cup French dressing

❏ 1 ❏ 2 ❏ 3

QUICK BROILED FILLETS

1/4 cup melted margarine	1 TBsp. parsley flakes
1 tsp. salt, dash of pepper	2 TBsp. lemon juice

❏ 1 ❏ 2 ❏ 3

MARINADE MOLOKAI

4 TBsp. steak sauce	1/2 cup pineapple juice

❏ 1 ❏ 2 ❏ 3

MARINADE CHINOIS

3 TBsp. orange juice	1 TBsp. parsley flakes
1 TBsp. salad oil	1 TBsp. lemon juice
1 TBsp. soy sauce	1/4 tsp. garlic powder
1 TBsp. ketchup	1/4 tsp. oregano

❏ 1 ❏ 2 ❏ 3

MARINADE OAHU

4 TBsp. salad oil	4 TBsp. lemon juice
4 TBsp. barbecue sauce	1 TBsp. onion flakes
4 TBsp. pineapple juice	1 tsp. salt

❏ 1 ❏ 2 ❏ 3

MARINADE FRANCAIS

1/2 cup French dressing	1 TBsp. onion flakes
1 TBsp. lemon juice	1 tsp. salt

❏ 1 ❏ 2 ❏ 3

ORIENTAL MARINADE

1/4 cup salad oil
3 TBsp. soy sauce

1/2 tsp. ginger
1 TBsp. brown sugar

❑ 1 ❑ 2 ❑ 3

AMAH MARINADE

1/4 cup orange juice
1 TBsp. lemon juice
2 TBsp. soy sauce
2 TBsp. salad oil

1 TBsp. parsley flakes
1/2 tsp. oregano
1/4 tsp. white pepper
1/4 tsp. garlic powder

❑ 1 ❑ 2 ❑ 3

PEPPERY FILLETS

1/4 cup salad oil
3 TBsp. lemon juice
1 TBsp. Worcestershire sauce

1/8 tsp. white pepper
4-5 dashes hot pepper sauce
1 tsp. salt

❑ 1 ❑ 2 ❑ 3

GRILLED WITH HERBS

1/2 cup white wine vinegar
1/2 tsp. rosemary
1/2 tsp. thyme

1/2 tsp. ground bay leaves
1/4 tsp. garlic powder

❑ 1 ❑ 2 ❑ 3

SPICY FISH BROIL

1/4 cup wine vinegar
4 TBsp. steak sauce
2 TBsp. ketchup

1/2 tsp. garlic powder
1/2 tsp. curry powder
1/2 tsp. salt

❑ 1 ❑ 2 ❑ 3

WINE MARINADE

1/2 cup dry white wine
1/4 cup salad oil
1 TBsp. lemon juice

1 tsp. rosemary
1 tsp. salt

❑ 1 ❑ 2 ❑ 3

❧ 4 ❧

Flaked Fish

The fish that may be used in the following recipes includes many of the previously cooked white-meated species. However, if you have no flaked fish, canned salmon may also be used. In recipes calling for a cup of flaked fish, use the 7 3/4-oz. can.

In a Casserole Dish or Loaf Pan

CRAB AND FISH LOAF

1/4 stick margarine   *1 can (6 oz.) crab*
1/2 cup diced onion   *1 cup flaked fish*
1 TBsp. flour   *Salt and pepper to taste*
1 cup milk, or as needed   *12 crushed soda crackers*

In a skillet saute onion in margarine until tender. Add flour, then milk, stirring until thickened. Stir in fish, crab and seasonings, turn into a loaf pan, cover with cracker crumbs and bake 20-25 minutes at 350 degrees.

❑ 1 ❑ 2 ❑ 3   832 calories

FISH/CHEESE CASSEROLE

1/4 stick margarine	1/2 cup grated cheese
1/2 cup diced celery	1 cup flaked fish
1/2 cup diced green pepper	1 TBsp. lemon juice
1 TBsp. flour	Salt and pepper to taste
1 cup milk, or as needed	1 cup fresh bread crumbs

In a skillet saute celery and green pepper in margarine until tender. Add flour and stir in milk until thickened.

Add cheese, fish, lemon juice and seasonings as desired, turn into a greased casserole dish, cover with bread crumbs and bake 20-25 minutes at 350 degrees.

❏ 1 ❏ 2 ❏ 3   842 calories

FISH N' SHRIMP BAKE

1 cup flaked fish	1/2 tsp. lemon pepper
1 can condensed cream of	2 TBsp. diced green onion
shrimp soup	12 crushed soda crackers
1 beaten egg	1/4 cup milk

Combine all ingredients in a greased loaf pan and bake 20-25 minutes at 350 degrees.

❏ 1 ❏ 2 ❏ 3   620 calories

FISH AND RICE BAKE

1/4 stick margarine	1 cup cooked rice
1/2 cup diced celery	1 can (8 oz.) tomato sauce
1/2 cup diced onion	1/2 cup milk
1 cup flaked fish	Salt and pepper to taste
	12 crushed soda crackers

In a skillet saute celery and onion in margarine until tender. Combine in a greased loaf pan with all but the crackers, which you sprinkle on top, and bake 20-25 minutes at 350 degrees.

❏ 1 ❏ 2 ❏ 3   852 calories

LO-CAL CASSEROLE

1/2 cup chicken bouillon	*1 can (4 oz.) mushroom pieces*
1 cup flaked fish	*1 TBsp. Worcestershire sauce*
1/2 cup Minute rice	*Salt and pepper to taste*
1/2 cup grated cheddar	*1 cup herb-seasoned croutons*

In a greased loaf pan combine all but the croutons, which you sprinkle on top, and bake 20-25 minutes at 350 degrees.

❏ 1 ❏ 2 ❏ 3   593 calories

BASIC FISH LOAF

1 cup flaked fish	*1/2 cup diced celery*
1 cup fresh bread crumbs	*1/4 tsp. lemon pepper*
1 beaten egg	*Salt to taste*
1/2 cup chicken bouillon	*12 crushed soda crackers*

Combine all but the crackers in a greased oven pan, sprinkle over with the crackers and bake 20-25 minutes at 350 degrees.

❏ 1 ❏ 2 ❏ 3   425 calories

COD AND EGG CASSEROLE

1/4 stick margarine	*2 beaten eggs*
1/2 cup diced onion	*1 TBsp. Worcestershire sauce*
1 cup flaked fish	*1 TBsp. parsley flakes*
1 cup soft bread crumbs	*Salt to taste*
	2 hard-boiled eggs, sliced

In a skillet saute onion in margarine until tender. In a greased casserole dish combine all but the eggs, which are placed on top, cover and bake 20-25 minutes at 350 degrees.

❏ 1 ❏ 2 ❏ 3   827 calories

CHEESE/TOMATO SANDWICH

1/2 cup flaked fish	*Salt and pepper to taste*
1 TBsp. diced radish	*4 tomato slices*
1 TBsp. mayonnaise	*2 slices toasted bread*
1 TBsp. sour cream	*2 slices cheese*

Mix together fish, radish, mayonnaise, sour cream and seasonings as desired.

Cut each slice of toast in half and place a tomato slice on each.

Spread cheese mixture over tomato slices to edge of the toast. Top each piece with half a slice of cheese, place on a cookie sheet and broil until cheese melts.

❏ 1 ❏ 2 ❏ 3   590 calories

❧ 5 ❧

Salt Cod and Lutefisk
(Plus Gravlax and Saviche)

Salt Cod—A Brush with American History

The continental shelf of the northeastern United States and eastern Canada extends for many miles out into the Atlantic in a relatively shallow bank before plummeting to the mid-ocean depths. The cold, plankton-rich waters support a great abundance of sea life, not the least of which is Atlantic cod.

The huge schools were heavily fished—unfortunately over-fished—and to the early settlers in colonial days provided a cheap and abundant source of protein. With no year-round refrigeration the cod were salted down to prevent spoilage and was a staple of the New England diet. Despite the prevalence of modern refrigeration, salt cod is still available in New England, although it is not so easily obtained in the Northwest.

A great many recipes evolved, and some of them are used to this day. Following is a sampling of some of those recipes. Specific quantities are listed in deference to a calorie count, but different proportions may be used as no doubt they were in colonial days. Oil for frying is not included in calorie counts.

The first task in preparation is to remove the salt, which is simply done by immersing the cod in cold, fresh water for a couple of days, changing the water from time to time.

If you don't find salt cod in your seafood store, you can easily make your own. Pacific, or true cod, is nearly identical to its Atlantic cousin and is prevalent in the Northwest.

If you'd like to sample the fare of our New England forefathers this is done using either non-iodized salt or rock salt. If you wish to sample a small amount to begin with put two or three fillets in a plastic refrigerator container. Salt them down—and don't skimp on the salt—cover and place in the refrigerator for a few days, or weeks as you desire.

After the salt has been removed, the flesh has a firmer texture and a different flavor—some say better—than fresh cod.

The following recipes were created with salt cod in mind, but they can be used with fresh cod as well.

COD WHITE SAUCE

1/2 lb. salt cod, cubed	*2 TBsp. flour*
1 cup milk, or to cover	*2 hard-boiled eggs*
1/2 stick margarine	*Salt and pepper to taste*

Simmer cod in milk until flaky. Melt margarine in a double boiler, stir in flour, add the milk and cod, stirring until thickened as desired, then add sliced hard-boiled eggs.

❏ 1 ❏ 2 ❏ 3   540 calories

OLD-FASHIONED CODFISH BALLS

1 cup salt cod, cooked and flaked	*1/4 stick melted margarine*
1 cup mashed potatoes	*Salt and pepper to taste*
1 beaten egg	*Crushed crackers as needed*
	Oil as needed for frying

Combine all ingredients except oil and crackers. Shape into balls, roll in the crushed crackers and fry in hot oil until browned. If the mixture isn't of a consistency to shape into balls, place by the spoonful onto a plate covered with crushed crackers, cover with crackers and fry as patties. Or, you may use more cod and potato in relation to the egg.

NOTE: For variations on this basic recipe add one of the following:
A tablespoon of lemon juice; A tablespoon of poultry seasoning and; a half cup of finely diced onion.

❏ 1 ❏ 2 ❏ 3   739 calories

CODFISH MAINE STYLE

3 strips of bacon, diced	*1 cup salt cod, cooked and flaked*
2 TBsp. flour	*2 hard-boiled eggs, chopped*
1 cup milk	*Salt and pepper to taste*

Fry bacon in skillet until crisp. Brown flour in bacon fat and stir in milk until it starts to thicken. Add fish, eggs and seasonings, stirring until hot. Serve over rice, boiled or mashed potatoes, or toast.

❏ 1 ❏ 2 ❏ 3   840 calories

NARAGANSETT CHOWDER

1/2 lb. salt pork, cubed	*2 bay leaves*
1 lb. salt cod, cubed	*2 cups diced potatoes*
	2 cups milk

In a saucepan fry the salt pork until it starts to brown. Add the remaining ingredients and simmer slowly until the potatoes are tender.

❏ 1 ❏ 2 ❏ 3   1,720 calories

CAPE COD CHOWDER

1/4 cup salt pork, cubed, or	*1 bay leaf*
4-5 slices diced bacon	*1 lb. salt cod, cubed*
1 cup diced onion	*3/4 cup milk*
1/2 cup water	*1 can (16 oz.) crushed*
2 cups diced potato	*tomatoes*
1/8 tsp. white pepper	*1/4 stick margarine*
	Salt to taste

In a large saucepan fry pork or bacon until tender, then remove. Remove fat as desired, then saute onion until tender. Add water, stir in potatoes, pepper and bay leaf. Bring to boil, reduce heat, cover and simmer until potatoes are done.

Add pork or bacon and cubed cod, heat to boiling, reduce heat to low, cover and simmer until fish flakes.

Discard bay leaf, add milk, crushed tomatoes, margarine, salt to taste and re-heat.

❏ 1 ❏ 2 ❏ 3   1,114 calories

Lutefisk

Oh, lutefisk, oh, lutefisk, how fragrant your aroma.
Oh, lutefisk, oh, lutefisk, you put me in a coma.
You smell so strong, you look like glue,
You taste just like an overshoe.
But lutefisk come Saturday, I think I'll eat you anyway.

Lutefisk, Scandinavia's gift to the world's cuisine, has never made it as big as hamburgers and pizza. However, it had a practical application in the old country where fish was plentiful but refrigeration was not. It was a method of preserving the fish for later use. Its primary attribute was practicability not palatability, although no true Scandihoovian would likely admit to the latter.

The fish, usually cod, was dried and then cured in a manner that kept it from spoiling for a considerable time. No one knows for sure who made the first lutefisk (which means "lye-fish"), but legend has it, as with so many inventions, it was accidental. A Scandinavian farmer had some cod stored in a shed, which caught fire and burned. Hoping to salvage what he could, he scraped away the ashes and found the fish had been transformed into the world's first lutefisk.

The following is a method—origin unknown—once employed. And while you may never make lutefisk from scratch, some insight into how it was accomplished should instill a greater appreciation for the convenience offered by your neighborhood seafood store.

9 lbs. dried fish	**1 2/3 lbs. baking soda**
2 lbs. slaked lime	**Water as needed**

1. Place the dried fish in a wooden receptacle and cover with cold water, changing the water every day for a week.

2. Make a solution of the lime, soda and 15 quarts of water, place the fish in the solution under weights to keep the pieces in position as they swell, and water as needed to keep them covered.

3. In about a week, or when sufficiently softened, take out, rinse thoroughly, and place in cold water for eight days, changing water daily for the first few days.

4. Cut in serving size pieces, remove skin, and it's ready.

One cooking method is to place the fish in cheesecloth, place in boiling water and cook for 10 to 15 minutes. A similar method is to put the fish in cold water, turn on the heat and when the water starts to boil the fish is done. It can be wrapped in foil and baked for around an hour at 350 degrees, or microwaved, covered, for 10 minutes or so.

Lutefisk is served with drawn butter or some type of sauce. A lingonberry sauce is traditional, or a cream sauce to which a bit of dry mustard has been added.

Gravlax (Gravad Lax)

This is another traditional Scandinavian recipe for curing raw fish, requiring a minimum of ingredients and time in preparation. If you are one of those who view with suspicion recipes that "cook" fish without using heat, such as sushi and saviche, you can experiment with a pound of fillets rather than committing four or five pounds of precious salmon or cod to an unknown fate.

4-5 lbs. of fillets, with skin,
  in 2 or more portions
1/2 cup coarse salt (or
  non-iodized table salt)

1/2 cup pepper, coarsely
  ground preferred
1/2 cup sugar
Fresh dill as needed

Mix salt, pepper and sugar together and rub it well into the fish. Spread dill across the bottom of a deep pan and lay a fillet on it, skin side down. Sprinkle dill on top of the fish. (If you don't have fresh dill mix two tablespoons of dried dillweed with the seasonings).

If there are just two fillets, lay the second on the first, skin side up, and lay a board on top with a pound or two of weight. If there are more than two fillets stack them one on top of the other, adding dill to each, with the top fillet skin side up. Put them in the refrigerator for a minimum of 24 hours.

Cut into slices for serving. Goes well with crackers, or dipped in an oil and vinegar dressing.

❏ 1 ❏ 2 ❏ 3

Saviche (ceviche)

The easiest of all party appetizers to prepare is saviche. It's simply raw fish "cooked" in either lemon or lime juice.

Cut a fillet of most any species of fish into bite-sized portions, place in a glass or plastic container, add some lime or lemon juice, and a few hours of time will do the rest. Sprinkle on salt, or none at all, according to your tastes.

It isn't necessary that the juice completely cover the fish, although the container should be covered and inverted a time or two, or shaken occasionally to insure that all the pieces are marinaded equally. Purists may insist on using the juice of real lemons or limes. However, the reconstituted variety will also do the job.

After marinading for a few hours it may be served as finger food. Or, with toothpicks, may be eaten with a variety of dips, which devotees of more traditional cooking methods may prefer.

❏ 1 ❏ 2 ❏ 3

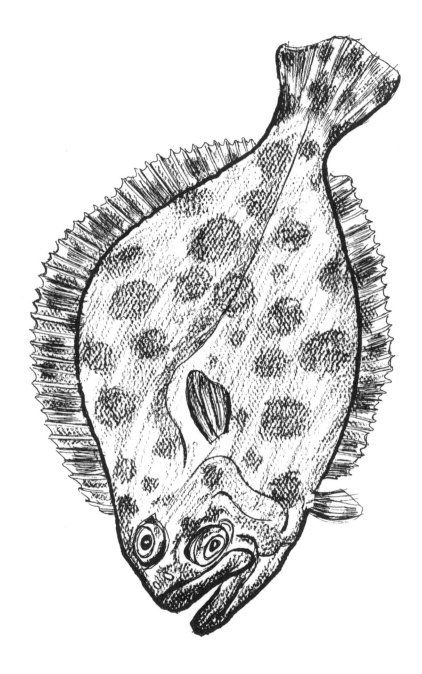

❧ 6 ☙

Halibut

Probably the most highly prized of all the bottom-dwelling fish is halibut. Its flesh has a fine, flaky texture, and a delicate taste that fairly shouts, "Don't mess me up using fancy recipes with their herbs and spices that destroy my flavor."

Although the recipes in this chapter specify halibut, feel free to substitute any of the other white-meated species.

In a Skillet

We must admit that when it comes to halibut we have a strong urge to go the simple route, the same as with a salmon steak. That is to say, heat up the skillet, add a dollop or two of butter or margarine, and listen to the sizzle of frying fish. Nevertheless, if you want to fancy things up a bit, following are a few suggestions.

In an Oven Pan

BASIC BAKED HALIBUT

1/2 lb. steaks or fillets
Salt and pepper to taste

1/2 stick melted butter or
margarine

Arrange fish in a greased oven pan, rub on seasonings, baste with butter or margarine and bake 20-25 minutes at 350 degrees.

❑ 1 ❑ 2 ❑ 3   600 calories

CHAMBERLIN'S SAVORY HALIBUT

1/2 lb. steaks or fillets
Salt and pepper to taste
1/4 stick margarine
1 can (4 oz.) mushroom pieces

1/2 cup sour cream
1 TBsp. cornstarch
1/4 cup sherry wine
Dash paprika (optional)

Season fish, place in a greased oven pan and bake 10 minutes at 350 degrees to partially cook. Remove.

Saute mushrooms in margarine, dissolve cornstarch in a little water and stir into mushrooms with sour cream and wine.

When thickened, pour over fish, sprinkle with paprika, cover and bake another 10 minutes at 350 degrees.

❑ 1 ❑ 2 ❑ 3   898 calories

HALIBUT WITH AN ORIENTAL TOUCH

1/2 lb. steaks or fillets
2 TBsp. olive oil
1/8 tsp. curry powder

2 TBsp. soy sauce
1/4 cup diced green onion
Salt and pepper to taste

Place fillets in a greased oven pan. Combine olive oil, curry powder and soy sauce, spoon over fish and let stand a half hour or more. Sprinkle over with diced onion and bake 20-25 minutes at 350 degrees. Season to taste when done.

❑ 1 ❑ 2 ❑ 3   454 calories

CREOLE HALIBUT

1/2 lb. steaks or fillets
1 can (8 oz.) tomato sauce
1 TBsp. flour

1/2 tsp. onion powder
Parmesan cheese as desired

Place fish in greased oven pan. Combine tomato sauce, flour and onion powder, pour over fish and bake 20 minutes at 350 degrees. Remove, sprinkle with parmesan cheese and place under broiler for a few moments until cheese starts to melt.

❑ 1 ❑ 2 ❑ 3   467 calories

WITH YOGURT AND CHEESE

1/4 cup diced green onion
1/2 cup sour cream
1/4 tsp. white pepper
1/4 tsp. dillweed

Salt to taste
1/2 lb. steaks or fillets
1 cup grated cheddar, or
  parmesan cheese as desired

Combine first five ingredients in a saucepan over low heat and stir until blended. Spread over fish and bake 20 minutes at 350 degrees. Sprinkle with cheese and broil a few moments.

❑ 1 ❑ 2 ❑ 3   436 calories

BAKED HALIBUT WITH LEMON

1/2 lb. steaks or fillets
2 TBsp. oil

1/4 cup lemon juice
1/2 tsp. salt, or as desired

Marinate fish in combined ingredients for a half hour or more and bake in a greased ovan pan 20-25 minutes at 350 degrees.

❏ 1 ❏ 2 ❏ 3   420 calories

CREAM CHEESE HALIBUT

1/4 stick margarine
1/2 cup grated carrot
1/4 cup diced green onion
1 pkg. (3 oz.) cream cheese

2 TBsp. lemon juice
1 TBsp. parsley flakes
1/4 tsp. white pepper
1/2 lb. steaks or fillets

Saute carrot and green onion in margarine until tender. Combine with cream cheese, lemon juice, parsley and pepper.

Arrange fillets in a greased oven pan, cover with vegetable mixture and bake 20-25 minutes at 350 degrees.

❏ 1 ❏ 2 ❏ 3   755 calories

ZESTY HALIBUT

1/2 lb. steaks or fillets
1/4 stick margarine
1/2 cup ketchup

1/4 cup diced onion
2 TBsp. vinegar
1 TBsp. Worcestershire sauce
1 TBsp. brown sugar

Place steaks or fillets in a greased oven pan, top each with a pat of butter and bake 10 minutes at 350 degrees. Remove.

Simmer remaining ingredients in a saucepan five minutes.

Pour sauce over fish and bake an additional 10 minutes at 350 degrees.

❏ 1 ❏ 2 ❏ 3   898 calories

HAUGE'S HALIBUT

1/3 cup oil
1 TBsp. Dijon mustard
2 TBsp. lemon juice

1 TBsp. onion flakes
Salt and pepper to taste
1/2 lb. steaks or fillets

Marinate fish in combined ingredients for a half hour or more and bake in a greased oven pan 20-25 minutes at 350 degrees.

❏ 1 ❏ 2 ❏ 3   480 calories

❧ 7 ❧

The Whole Fish

In days of yore, as a Boy Scout hiking the Cascade Mountains of Washington, I'd carry some string and a hook in my packsack. Using a bit of bacon or a piece of cheese for bait, and a small branch from a tree or a length of brush for a rod, it was possible to catch a mess of unsophisticated trout from those little-visited streams of the 1920s. Plopped into a mess kit with sizzling bacon grease, the resulting dish yielded an aroma and flavor beyond the ability of the world's finest chefs to duplicate.

Although many years have gone by, our cooking method for pan-size trout remains basically the same. The principal differences are the addition of a coating such as flour, or cornmeal, a Teflon skillet instead of a World War I Army mess kit, plus margarine instead of bacon grease in deference to the cholesterol which hadn't been invented yet in those innocent years.

There was no problem finding room, even in a folding mess kit, for the trout from those mountain streams. But, how do you pan-fry a fat trout that's 12 or more inches long? It's a bit too small to fillet or to stuff and bake, and frying in the round would likely leave the center underdone.

One solution would be to fry it on both sides, then separate it by running a spatula along the backbone and frying the two halves, skin side up, for a couple or three more minutes.

Or, instead of frying, simply lay it in a greased oven pan and bake for 20 minutes, or so, at 350 degrees.

Cooking in aluminum foil is another method that's simply great with larger trout—or other fish for that matter. That's especially true if you've been out on a stream fishing, far from your camper or cabin. Remember to bring along, in addition to the foil, salt and pepper, onions and bacon. Let a campfire burn down to a good bed of coals, lay the seasoned fish in a square of foil, surround it with sliced onion and bacon, seal it well and bury it in the coals. You may also include a few slices of lemon. The cooking time will have to be left to your instincts, but if you open the foil and don't find a banquet you obviously didn't work hard enough for those fish.

Of course, this cooking method isn't limited to a campfire. You can do it at home in the oven or over glowing charcoal.

An objection might be that when the fish is done the onion and bacon are likely to remain under-cooked. Out in the woods, with appetites as big as all outdoors, this tends to be a minor consideration. But at home it's another matter to diet-conscious diners accustomed to crisply fried bacon. If you're cooking in an oven with an overhead broiler, lay the onion slices on top of the fish, then cover them with bacon before sealing. Lay the fish in a pan and bake 30 minutes or so, depending on size, at 350 degrees. Then, with the top four to five inches below the heating element, broil for six to eight minutes.

Imaginative cooks will likely try out other seasoning combinations omitting the onion and bacon. Suggestions would include, along with salt, onion and garlic powder, seasoned salt, lemon pepper, tarragon, and the list goes on.

It isn't necessary to remove the scales from trout or salmon, although they are undesirable on fish with coarser scales. However, if you do wish to remove the scales on a salmon it can easily be done by laying it on the grass and then directing a strong stream with a garden hose from the tail forward.

Grilled Trout

Trout in the pound or more size, too big for pan-frying, can also be grilled over the coals. Handling a fish of this size can be facilitated by cutting two strips, a foot or two long and an inch or so wide, from aluminum foil. Lay the fish on the foil, one near each end, and twist the ends together. Thus you can easily lift the fish onto the grill and off again.

Before grilling, the seasonings of your choice should be rubbed into the fish's cavity. That's really all you need to do. However, a variety of marinades may be used as a basting sauce. Following is one suggestion, but you will find many more in the chapter on "Sauces and Marinades", as well as the chapter on "Salmon Steaks and Fillets."

1/2 stick of melted margarine
1/2 tsp. grated lemon peel
1 TBsp. lemon juice

1/4 tsp. salt
1/8 tsp, each pepper, paprika
and garlic powder

Baked or Roasted Salmon

Salmon in the four to six or seven-pound range are fine for roasting. One method is to rub with seasonings, brush with melted butter or margarine and bake at 350 degrees for 40 to 50 minutes. You may, if you wish, baste with butter or margarine from time to time, or simply lay a few strips of bacon on the fish and let the melting fat do the basting for you.

Or, simply cover and roast ten minutes for each inch of thickness in a 400-degree oven, adding whatever seasonings are desired afterward.

If you want to get a bit fancier you can fill the cavity with a variety of stuffings as with turkey. If you stuff the fish you'd best leave the head on to help hold in the stuffing.

Following are stuffing recipes that are adequate for salmon up to six or seven pounds. The fish should first be rubbed with seasonings inside and out, then stuffed, closed with skewers, laid on a greased oven pan, covered with bacon strips if you want to go this route, and baked 50 minutes to an hour at 350 degrees.

YEE'S YOGURT STUFFING

1/2 cup diced celery	*2 cups fresh bread crumbs*
1/2 cup diced onion	*1 tsp. paprika*
1/2 stick margarine	*1/2 cup yogurt or sour cream*
1 lemon	*1/2 tsp. salt*

Saute celery and onion in margarine, grate lemon rind, chop up rest of the lemon and combine with remaining ingredients.

❑ 1 ❑ 2 ❑ 3

STUFFING A LA HANSEN

1/2 cup diced onion	*2 cups fresh bread crumbs*
1/2 cup diced celery	*4 TBsp. minced parsley*
1/2 stick margarine	*1 can (4 oz.) mushroom pieces*
1/2 cup diced chicken	*4 slices bacon, diced*

Saute veggies in margarine and combine with other ingredients.

NOTE: The remaining recipes follow the same instructions.

❑ 1 ❑ 2 ❑ 3

CARL'S CORNBREAD STUFFING

1 cup diced onion
1 cup diced celery
1/2 stick margarine

1 TBsp. lemon juice
1/2 tsp. salt
2 cups soft bread crumbs
1 cup crumbled cornbread

❑ 1 ❑ 2 ❑ 3

ROY'S RICE/MUSHROOM STUFFING

1 stick margarine
1 cup diced onion
1 cup diced celery

1 can (4 oz.) mushroom pieces
2 cups cooked rice
1/2 tsp. each salt, thyme, sage

❑ 1 ❑ 2 ❑ 3

BOB'S BREAD STUFFING

1 stick margarine
1 cup diced onion
1 cup diced celery

3 cups fresh bread crumbs
1/2 tsp. each salt, pepper,
  thyme and sage

❑ 1 ❑ 2 ❑ 3

Joyce Herbst with a big Chinook salmon from Tillamook Bay, Oregon.

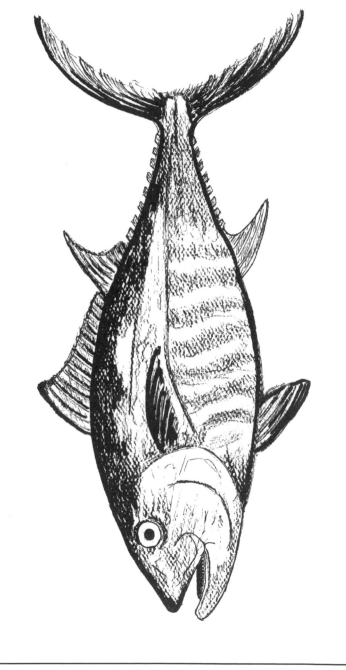

🌿 8 🌿

Tuna

This is one of the best known of all fish that swim the world's oceans. Because of its popularity in a variety of dishes, it has great commercial value. And, in addition to its welcome presence on the table, it is highly prized by sports anglers due to its hard-fighting qualities at the end of a line.

Most tuna comes to us in a can, mostly in the 6 or 6 1/2-ounce size. So, note that in all the following recipes this popular size can is used.

If you're looking for more variety than will be found here, turn to the chapter on canned salmon. In most recipes they are pretty much interchangeable.

In a Casserole or Oven Pan

BASIC TUNA CASSEROLE

1 cup coarse cracker crumbs	*1 can tuna*
1/2 cup finely diced celery	*1/2 stick melted margarine*
1/2 cup finely diced onion	*2 beaten eggs*
1 TBsp. parsley flakes	*Salt and pepper to taste*

Combine all ingredients, turn into a greased casserole dish, cover and bake 30 minutes at 350 degrees.

❑ 1 ❑ 2 ❑ 3   1,015 calories

CLASSIC TUNA CASSEROLE

1 cup cooked macaroni	*1 can cream of celery soup*
1 can tuna	*2 TBsp. onion flakes*
	1 cup fresh bread crumbs

Combine first four ingredients in a greased casserole dish, cover with bread crumbs and bake 30 minutes at 350 degrees.

❑ 1 ❑ 2 ❑ 3   620 calories

TUNA/VEGETABLE CASSEROLE

1 cup cooked carrots, diced	1 can cream of mushroom soup
1 can tuna	1 cup mashed potatoes
1 cup cooked peas	Salt and pepper to taste

Combine carrots, tuna and peas in a greased casserole dish. Spoon over with undiluted soup, cover with mashed potatoes, season to taste, and bake 20 minutes at 350 degrees.

❏ 1 ❏ 2 ❏ 3   550 calories

FANCY VEGGIE/TUNA CASSEROLE

1/2 cup diced potatoes	2 TBsp. flour
1/2 cup diced carrots	1 cup milk, or as needed
1/2 cup diced onion	Salt and pepper to taste
1 cup cooked peas	1 can tuna
1/4 stick margarine	1 cup fresh bread crumbs

In a saucepan boil potatoes, carrots and onion until tender. Discard water and add peas. In a saucepan or double boiler make a white sauce with margarine, flour, milk and seasonings.
Combine veggies and white sauce with tuna in a greased casserole dish, top with crumbs and bake 20 minutes at 350 degrees.

❏ 1 ❏ 2 ❏ 3   792 calories

TUNA QUICHE WITH CHEESE

1/4 stick margarine	1 cup milk, or as needed
2 TBsp. flour	2 eggs, separated
Salt and pepper to taste	1 cup grated cheese
4-5 dashes hot pepper sauce	1 can tuna
1 TBsp. Worcestershire sauce	

In a skillet melt margarine, add flour and seasonings and slowly pour in milk, stirring until thickened.
Stir egg yokes into the sauce, blend in the cheese and fish, then fold in the stiffly beaten egg whites.
Pour the mixture into a greased casserole dish, place in a pan with water and bake 30 minutes at 350 degrees.

❏ 1 ❏ 2 ❏ 3   1,060 calories

TUNA/PEAS/TOMATO COMBO

1 cup cooked rice
1 cup cooked peas
1 can tuna
1/2 cup diced onion
1/4 stick margarine
1 TBsp. flour

1 cup milk
1 TBsp. Worcestershire sauce
Salt and pepper to taste
1 sliced tomato
1/2 cup grated cheese

Combine rice, peas and tuna in a greased casserole dish.

In a skillet saute onion in margarine until tender. Add flour and stir in milk until thickened. Add Worcestershire sauce and seasonings, then pour over tuna mixture.

Arrange tomato slices on top. Cover with grated cheese and bake 20 minutes at 350 degrees.

❑ 1 ❑ 2 ❑ 3   1,026 calories

IMPROBABLE TUNA PIE

1 can tuna
1/2 cup grated cheese
2 TBsp. mayonnaise

1 cup milk
1/2 cup baking mix
2 eggs
Salt to taste

In a bowl combine first three ingredients.

Mix remaining ingredients in a blender turned on high for 10-15 seconds. Combine everything in a greased casserole dish and bake 30 minutes at 400 degrees.

❑ 1 ❑ 2 ❑ 3   1,025 calories

IMPOSSIBLE TUNA PIE

1 can tuna
1/2 cup grated cheese
1 pkg. (3 oz.) cream cheese
3 TBsp. diced green onions
1 TBsp. chopped piemento

1 cup milk
1/2 cup baking mix
2 eggs
Salt to taste
Dash of nutmeg

In a bowl combine first five ingredients,

Mix remaining ingredients in a blender turned on high for 10-15 seconds. Combine everything in a greased casserole dish and bake 30 minutes at 400 degrees.

❑ 1 ❑ 2 ❑ 3   980 calories

NUTTY CHOW MEIN TUNA

1/4 stick margarine
1/2 cup diced onion
1/2 cup diced celery
1/4 cup diced green pepper
1 can tuna

1 can cream of mushroom soup
1/4 cup chopped nuts (walnuts,
pecans, etc.)
1 can (3 oz.) chow mein
noodles

In a skillet saute veggies in margarine until tender, and in a bowl combine with remaining ingredients except noodles.

Spread half the noodles in bottom of a greased casserole dish, pour in the tuna mix, top with remaining noodles and bake 30 minutes at 350 degrees.

❑ 1 ❑ 2 ❑ 3   1,079 calories

In a Saucepan or Skillet

TUNA CHOWDER

1 cup cubed, cooked potatoes
4 slices diced bacon
1/2 cup diced onion
1/4 tsp. thyme

1 can (16 oz.) crushed tomatoes
2 cups milk
2 cans tuna
Salt and pepper to taste

Boil potatoes until tender and discard water.

Fry bacon in a kettle or deep skillet, then saute onion until tender in whatever fat you wish to retain.

Add remaining ingredients and heat to a simmer.

❑ 1 ❑ 2 ❑ 3   1,227 calories

TUNA/SPAGHETTI DINNER

1/4 stick margarine
1/2 cup diced onion
1/2 cup diced celery
1 TBsp. flour
1 can (8 oz.) tomato sauce

1 can tuna
1 TBsp. parsley flakes
1/4 tsp. garlic powder
Salt and pepper to taste
1/4 cup sherry (optional)

In a skillet saute onion and celery in margarine until tender. Stir in flour, add remaining ingredients, stir until thickened and hot, and serve over spaghetti.

❑ 1 ❑ 2 ❑ 3   567 calories

BAYOU TUNA

1 can (4 oz.) mushroom pieces
1/4 stick margarine
1/4 cup diced green pepper
1/2 cup diced onion
2 TBsp. flour

Dash pepper
3-4 dashes hot pepper sauce
2 TBsp. ketchup
1 can tuna
Cooked rice as desired

Drain mushrooms and add liquid to water to make 1/2 cup.

In a skillet saute green pepper and onion in margarine until tender, then add mushrooms.

Add flour plus mushroom liquid and water, stirring until it starts to thicken. Add remaining ingredients, stirring until thickened and hot. Serve over rice.

❑ 1 ❑ 2 ❑ 3   536 calories

TUNA CAKES FOR TWO

1 can tuna
1 cup mashed potatoes
1 beaten egg

1/4 cup chopped green onion
Salt and pepper to taste
Oil as needed for frying

Combine ingredients and spoon onto a hot greased skillet.

❑ 1 ❑ 2 ❑ 3   691 calories

SWEET AND SOUR TUNA

1 can (8 oz.) pineapple
   chunks
1/4 cup diced green pepper
1/4 cup diced celery
1/4 cup vinegar

1/4 cup water
1 TBsp. soy sauce
2 TBsp. cornstarch
1 can tuna

In a saucepan or skillet over low heat combine pineapple and juice, peppers, celery, vinegar, water and soy sauce.

Stir corn starh into a bit of water and add to contents of skillet or saucepan, stirring until it starts to thicken, add tuna and stir until heated. NOTE: Some tastes prefer the peppers and celery to be crisp. Others may wish to continue simmering until they soften.

❑ 1 ❑ 2 ❑ 3   324 calories

In a Sandwich

TRADITIONAL TUNA SANDWICH

1 can tuna
1/4 cup diced sweet pickle
2 hard-boiled eggs, diced

2 TBsp. mayonnaise, more or
   less according to taste
Salt and pepper to taste

Use as a sandwich filler with lettuce and tomatoes as desired.

❑ 1 ❑ 2 ❑ 3   600 calories

ROBIN'S CURRIED TUNA

1 can tuna
2 TBsp. mayonnaise

1/8 tsp. curry powder
1/4 cup raisins
1/4 cup diced apples

The foregoing amounts may be changed to suit individual tastes. But take care with the curry, it has a potent flavor.

❑ 1 ❑ 2 ❑ 3   600 calories

GARDEN TUNA SANDWICH

1 can tuna
1/2 cup grated zucchini
1/4 cup grated carrot
1 TBsp. ketchup

2 TBsp. mayonnaise
1 TBsp. lemon juice
Salt and pepper to taste

Excellent on buttered toast with lettuce, or may be combined with lettuce and tomato to make a salad.

❑ 1 ❑ 2 ❑ 3   444 calories

TUNA MEXICANA

1 can tuna
2 TBsp. finely diced pickle
1/4 cup finely diced cucumber
1/2 cup crushed Fritos

4 TBsp. mayonnaise
2 TBsp. lemon juice
4-5 dashes hot pepper sauce
Salt to taste

❑ 1 ❑ 2 ❑ 3   699 calories

TUNA ITALIANO

1 can tuna
4-5 ripe olives, diced
1/4 cup chopped cashews

1 TBsp. lemon juice
1 TBsp. mayonnaise
Salt and pepper to taste

❑ 1 ❑ 2 ❑ 3   728 calories

TUNABURGERS

1 can tuna
1 cup fresh bread crumbs
1 beaten egg
1/2 cup diced celery

1 TBsp. onion flakes
2 TBsp. mayonnaise
1 TBsp. flour
1 TBsp. lemon juice

Combine all ingredients, form into patties and fry on a greased skillet. Put on hamburger buns, or eat as is.

❑ 1 ❑ 2 ❑ 3   580 calories

TUNA/OLIVE OPEN FACE

1 can tuna
4-5 ripe olives, diced
2 TBsp. mayonnaise

4 slices toast
4 slices cheese

Combine tuna, olives and mayonnaise. Spread over four slices of toast, lay a slice of cheese on each and place under broiler until cheese melts. Toast may be buttered, or not, to your taste.

❏ 1 ❏ 2 ❏ 3   1,020 calories

TWO-IN-ONE TUNA SANDWICH

1 can tuna
2 TBsp. mayonnaise
1 TBsp. finely diced onion
1 TBsp. finely diced celery
1 TBsp. Worcestershire sauce
4 slices bread, or as needed

2 eggs
2 TBsp. milk
2 TBsp. oil
1 tsp. sugar
Salt and pepper to taste

Combine tuna, mayonnaise, onion, celery and Worcestershire sauce and use as a traditional sandwich filling.

To take the second step, after making the sandwiches, beat together the eggs, milk, oil, sugar and salt, pour onto a pie plate, soak sandwiches on both sides and place on a cookie sheet.

Bake 20 minutes at 350 degrees, or until golden brown.

❏ 1 ❏ 2 ❏ 3   1,035 calories

TUNA/MUSHROOM OPEN FACE

1/4 stick margarine
2 TBsp. flour
3/4 cup milk
1 can tuna
1 can (4 oz.) mushroom pieces

1 TBsp. Worcestershire sauce
4-5 dashes hot pepper sauce
1 TBsp. lemon juice
Salt and pepper to taste
1/2 cup grated cheddar

In a skillet melt margarine, add flour and stir in milk until thickened. Add remaining ingredients, except cheese, and re-heat. Spoon on top of bread slices, top with grated cheese and broil until cheese melts.

NOTE: If more thickening is needed, use a bit of cornstarch. Also, you may skip the cheese and use over rice or pasta.

❏ 1 ❏ 2 ❏ 3   733 calories

Fresh Albacore

Most of the seafood used in recipes elsewhere in this book is commonly available in supermarkets or seafood stores. Not so, fresh albacore tuna.

Albacore is one of the most highly prized of the various tuna species, not only for its superior table qualities but for the strong fight it puts up on a sports angler's tackle.

Traveling in a counter-clockwise circle around the North Pacific rim following the Japanese Current, albacore appear from 50 to 100 miles, or so, off the Washington-Oregon coast in late summer and early fall. However, not every year. Some years they're too far off shore to be reached by sport fishing boats on a one or two-day run. But occasionally they'll come in close enough to make an unexpected and exciting catch for salmon anglers. Much depends on the vagaries of the current, as well as the unpredictable effects of El Nino, a warm current off South America's Pacific Coast.

They have been intercepted for many years by the commercial fishing fleet. However, in the 1960s a newer and swifter generation of sports charter boats were developed which were able to get up on the plane and could occasionally reach the tuna by leaving in the early A.M., or on two-day overnight trips. With no limit on the number that could be taken, successful anglers naturally wanted to know how best to prepare these prized fish. All of the following recipes are from "Information Booklet No. 5" published by the Washington Department of Fisheries, now the Department of Fish and Wildlife.

The following recipes will not include a calorie count due to the varying amounts of fish that may be used. But, what the heck, forget about calories if you're enjoying fresh albacore.

POACHED ALBACORE

1. Arrange loins in a pan at least two inches deep.

2. In a saucepan combine one quart water, 1/2 cup vinegar, two teaspoons salt, one bay leaf, one medium sized onion and one carrot. Heat to simmering and pour over fish.

3. Cover the pan with foil and place in a 400-degree oven for 10-15 minutes. Carefully lift from the poaching liquid and chill.

NOTE: Poached albacore makes a fine cold entree, or may be substituted in any recipe calling for canned tuna.

❏ 1 ❏ 2 ❏ 3

TUNA BROILED WITH BACON

Bacon slices	*Freshly ground black pepper*
Split garlic cloves	*Seasoned salt*
Melted margarine	*Lemon wedges*

Cut the loin across the grain into one-inch thick slices and rub both sides with garlic, or sprinkle with garlic powder. Wrap a bacon slice around each loin and secure with a toothpick.

Place on a foil-lined greased oven pan, brush with butter or margarine, season with pepper and seasoned salt and broil for five minutes about four inches from heat. Turn, brushing second side with butter and seasonings. Broil until fish flakes with a fork and serve with lemon wedges.

❑ 1 ❑ 2 ❑ 3

ALBACORE BAKED IN FOIL

Albacore lends itself to this simple cooking method. Sprinkle over the fish whatever seasonings you desire such as salt, pepper, seafood seasoning, oregano, onion or garlic powder, lemon juice, sherry or other white wine, and butter. Cover tightly with foil.

Baking time is a variable depending on size of the loin, however, 30-35 minutes at 350 degrees would be in the ballpark.

You might want to open it up and check, then broil another few minutes if necessary; or brown it a bit.

❑ 1 ❑ 2 ❑ 3

BARBECUED ALBACORE

1 stick margarine　　　　　*4 TBsp. lemon juice*
1 minced garlic clove　　　*2 TBsp. parsley flakes*
Salt and pepper to taste

Prepare basting sauce by melting margarine in a small pan and stirring in garlic, lemon juice and parsley.

Arrange loins on grill over coals and cook until fish flakes, basting several times. Salt and pepper as desired.

❑ 1 ❑ 2 ❑ 3

FRIED FINGERS OF ALBACORE

1/2 cup flour　　　　　　*Oil as needed*
2 beaten eggs　　　　　　*Salt and pepper*
1 cup cracker crumbs　　*Tartar sauce*

Cut albacore into strips about three inches long and 1/2 inch thick. Dip in flour, then beaten egg, and roll in cracker crumbs. Fry in deep fat heated to 370 degrees for about three minutes or until golden brown. Drain on paper towels, season with salt and pepper and serve with tartar sauce as desired.

❑ 1 ❑ 2 ❑ 3

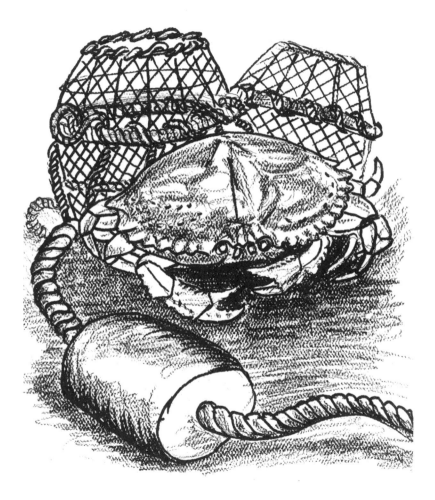

❧ 9 ❧

Crabs

Crabs are purchased in the shell with the probable intent of cracking open and eating the meat as is, usually with drawn butter or margarine, or perhaps some type of sauce.

A can, however, is the likely source of crab meat used in the following recipes. Or, you may use imitation crab. If so, figure on a cup of imitation crab to one 6-ounce can.

On Top of the Stove

EASY CRAB CAKES

1 cup crab, or imitation crab	1/2 tsp. prepared mustard
8 crushed soda crackers	1/2 tsp. seafood seasoning
1 TBsp. diced green onion	1 tsp. Worcestershire sauce
1 TBsp. finely diced celery	1 TBsp. mayonnaise

In a bowl combine all ingredients, form into patties and fry in a hot, greased skillet.

❏ 1 ❏ 2 ❏ 3   245 calories

FANCY CRAB CAKES

2 cups crab, or imitation crab	1 TBsp. Worcesterershire sauce
1/4 cup diced green onions	1/3 cup flour
2 TBsp. parsley flakes	2 tsp. baking powder
2 beaten eggs	1/2 tsp. salt

In a bowl mix the crab with the onion, parsley, eggs and Worcestershire sauce. Sift the flour, baking powder and salt into the crab mixture, form into patties or drop by the spoonful onto a hot, greased skillet.

❏ 1 ❏ 2 ❏ 3   552 calories

CRAB AND SCRAMBLED EGG SANDWICH

1 can (6 oz.) crab meat   4 slices bread, or as needed
2 eggs   Salt and pepper to taste

In a greased skillet scramble crab and eggs together and use as filling for a sandwich. The bread may be buttered, or spread with mayonnaise, according to your taste.

❏ 1 ❏ 2 ❏ 3   415 calories

CRAB NEWBERG

1/4 stick margarine   1 cup milk, half and half or
2 TBsp. flour   non-dairy liquid creamer
1/4 tsp. salt, or to taste   2 beaten egg yokes
1/4 tsp. nutmeg   1/4 cup dry white wine
3-4 drops hot pepper sauce   1 can (6 oz.) crab meat

Melt margarine in a saucepan or double boiler, add flour, salt, nutmeg and pepper sauce, then stir in milk until thickened.
Beat egg yokes and stir into sauce. Add flaked crab and wine, continuing to stir until heated. Serve over hot rice. Don't discard egg whites. Use with Salmon Bisque, page 143.

❏ 1 ❏ 2 ❏ 3   730 calories

CRAB CHOW MEIN

1/2 stick margarine   1 handful bean sprouts
1 cup diced celery   1 can (6 oz.) crab meat
1 cup diced onion   1 can cream of mushroom soup
1 cup diced green pepper   Chow mein noodles as desired

In a skillet saute first three veggies in margarine until tender. Add bean sprouts, crab and soup, simmer for a few minutes and serve over chow mein noodles.

❏ 1 ❏ 2 ❏ 3   825 calories

In the Oven

IMPOSSIBLE CRAB PIE

1 can (6 oz.) crab meat	1 cup milk
1/2 cup grated cheese	1/2 cup biscuit mix
1 pkg. (3 oz.) cream cheese	2 eggs
1/4 cup diced green onion	Salt to taste
1 jar (2 oz.) chopped pimento	Dash of nutmeg

Combine crab, grated cheese, softened cream cheese, green onion and pimento in a greased casserole dish.

Place remaining ingredients in a blender and turn on high for 15 seconds, then mix with crab and cheese.

Place casserole dish in a pan with water and bake 40 minutes at 350 degrees.

❏ 1 ❏ 2 ❏ 3   1,011 calories

CRAB N' TOMATO CASSEROLE

1 can (6 oz.) crab meat	1/2 cup grated cheese
1 can condensed tomato soup	12 crushed soda crackers
3 TBsp. mayonnaise	

Combine first four ingredients in a greased casserole dish, top with crushed soda crackers and bake 30 minutes at 350 degrees.

❏ 1 ❏ 2 ❏ 3   921 calories

CRAB N' CHEESE CASSEROLE

1/4 stick margarine	1 can (4 oz.) mushroom pieces
2 TBsp. flour	1/2 cup uncooked instant rice
1 cup chicken bouillon	1 cup grated cheddar cheese
1 can (6 oz.) crab meat	1/2 tsp. garlic powder
1/2 cup diced celery	Salt to taste

Melt margarine in a skillet, stir in flour and slowly add bouillon, stirring until thickened. Remove from heat.

In a greased casserole dish combine remaining ingredients, add bouillon and flour mixture and bake 30 minutes at 350 degrees.

❏ 1 ❏ 2 ❏ 3   903 calories

CRAB CUPCAKES

1 can (6 oz.) crab meat	1 TBsp. parsley flakes
2 beaten eggs	2 TBsp. biscuit mix
1 TBsp. soy sauce	1/2 tsp. salt, or to taste
1/4 cup diced green onion	1/4 cup oil

Combine ingredients and spoon into individual greased casserole dishes or cupcake tin. Place in a pan with water and bake 30 minutes at 350 degrees. Makes six cupcakes.

❏ 1 ❏ 2 ❏ 3   548 calories

CRAB N' CHESTNUTS CASSEROLE

1/2 cup uncooked instant rice	1/2 cup grated cheese
1 can (6 oz.) crab meat	1 can (4 oz.) mushroom pieces,
1 can cream of mushroom soup	including the liquid
1/2 can (8 oz.) water chestnuts	4-5 dashes hot pepper sauce

Combine all ingredients in a greased casserole dish and bake 30 minutes at 350 degrees. Use the other half can of water chestnuts in the recipe for Shrimp and Ham Bake.

❏ 1 ❏ 2 ❏ 3   748 calories

PETERSON'S PRIDE

1/4 stick margarine	Salt and pepper to taste
1/2 cup diced celery	1 cup milk
1/2 cup diced onion	1/2 cup grated cheese
1 TBsp. flour	1 can (6 oz.) crab meat
1 TBsp. parsley flakes	1 cup cooked macaroni

In a skillet saute celery and onion in margarine until tender. Add flour, parsley and seasonings slowly stirring in milk until thickened. Combine with remaining ingredients in a greased casserole dish and bake 30 minutes at 350 degrees.

❏ 1 ❏ 2 ❏ 3   822 calories

CRAB N' MUSHROOM CASSEROLE

1 can (6 oz.) crab meat	1 cup cooked peas
1 can cream of mushroom soup	1 cup fresh bread crumbs
1 can (4 oz.) mushroom pieces	

Combine ingredients in a greased casserole dish, cover with bread crumbs and bake 30 minutes at 350 degrees.

❏ 1 ❏ 2 ❏ 3   598 calories

CRAB N' SHRIMP CASSEROLE

1/4 stick margarine	*1 can (4 oz.) shrimp*
1/2 cup diced celery	*1 TBsp. mayonnaise*
1/2 cup diced onion	*1 TBsp. Worcestershire sauce*
1/4 cup diced green pepper	*Salt and pepper to taste*
1 can (6 oz.) crab meat	*1 cup fresh bread crumbs*

In a skillet saute veggies in margarine until tender. Combine with remaining ingredients in a greased casserole dish, cover with bread crumbs and bake 30 minutes at 350 degrees.

❏ 1 ❏ 2 ❏ 3   828 calories

A trap full of king crabs from Olga Bay, Kodiak Island.

❧ 10 ☙

Shrimp

Along with tuna, shrimp is probably the most popular non-fruit or vegetable component of salads. However, tasty shrimp may also serve as the prime ingredient in an entree dish.

This popular crustacean may be taken as a recreational endeavor in the Northwest, but the waters in which they are found are limited, and the seasons which they may be legally taken are short. As a result, most shrimp finds its way to the table from a supermarket shelf in a can, or fresh, but cooked, from a seafood store. The important thing is that they are available the year-round.

NOTE: Shrimp from the deli or from the seafood counter of your supermarket tends to be larger, and less closely packed, than shrimp in a can. As a result, in the following recipes one cup of fresh shrimp may be considered as equal to a 4-oz. can. Also, you may use half of a 17 1/2-oz. can of peas in recipes calling for a cup of cooked peas.

In the oven

SHRIMP AND HAM BAKE

1/4 stick margarine	*1 cup cooked shrimp*
1/2 cup diced celery	*1 cup cooked peas*
1/2 cup diced onion	*1/2 can (8 oz.) water chestnuts*
1/2 cup diced ham	*1/2 cup chicken bouillon*
	Salt and pepper to taste

In a skillet saute veggies in margarine until tender.

Combine all ingredients in a greased casserole dish and bake 30 minutes at 350 degrees. Use the remaining half can of water chestnuts from the Crab 'n Chestnuts casserole and the remaining peas in the following recipe, or both in a tossed salad.

❑ 1 ❑ 2 ❑ 3   632 calories

SHRIMP AND CRAB DELIGHT

1 cup cooked peas	*2 TBsp. mayonnaise*
1/2 cup diced celery	*1/2 tsp. salt, or to taste*
1 cup cooked shrimp	*1 cup grated cheese*
1 can (6 oz.) crab	*1 cup fresh bread crumbs*

Combine all but the crumbs in a greased casserole dish, sprinkle over with the crumbs and bake 30 minutes at 375 degrees.

❑ 1 ❑ 2 ❑ 3   830 calories

SHIRLEY'S SHRIMP BAKE

1/4 stick margarine	*1/2 cup grated cheese*
1/2 cup diced onion	*1 cup cooked rice*
1/2 cup diced green pepper	*1 cup cooked shrimp*
1 can cream of mushroom soup	*1/2 cup slivered almonds*

In a skillet saute onion and green pepper in margarine until tender. Combine in a greased casserole dish with other ingredients, sprinkle nuts on top and bake 30 minutes at 350 degrees.

❑ 1 ❑ 2 ❑ 3   955 calories, w/o nuts

CAPTAIN BILLY'S SHRIMP BAKE

1 cup cooked shrimp	*1 TBsp. mayonnaise*
1/2 can cream of mushroom soup	*1/2 cup grated cheese*
1 cup cooked pasta	

Combine all ingredients in a greased casserole dish and bake 30 minutes at 350 degrees.

❑ 1 ❑ 2 ❑ 3   690 calories

SHRIMP AND SHERRY BAKE

1/4 stick margarine	*2 TBsp. mayonnaise*
1/2 cup diced onion	*1/4 cup sherry*
1/2 cup diced celery	*1 cup cooked shrimp*
2 cups fresh bread crumbs	*Salt and pepper to taste*

In a skillet saute onion and celery in margarine until tender. Combine with other ingredients in a greased casserole dish and bake 30 minutes at 350 degrees.

❑ 1 ❑ 2 ❑ 3   722 calories

SHRIMP QUICHE

1 cup cooked shrimp	*1 can condensed shrimp soup*
2 eggs, separated	*(or cheddar cheese soup)*
1 cup fresh bread crumbs	*8 crushed soda crackers*

In a bowl combine shrimp, beaten egg yolks, crumbs and soup. Beat egg whites and fold into shrimp mixture. Turn into a greased casserole dish, cover with crushed soda crackers, place in a pan with water and bake 30 minutes at 350 degrees.

❑ 1 ❑ 2 ❑ 3   723 calories

In a Skillet or Saucepan

HOT SHRIMP CURRY ON RICE

1/4 stick margarine	*1/4 tsp. cayenne*
1/2 cup diced celery	*1/4 tsp. curry*
1/2 cup diced onion	*1/2 cup milk*
1 TBsp. flour	*1 cup cooked shrimp*

In a skillet saute celery and onion in margarine until tender. Add flour, seasonings and milk, stirring until thickened. Add shrimp, stir until hot. Serve over rice.

❑ 1 ❑ 2 ❑ 3   500 calories

JASMINE'S JAMBALAYA

1/4 stick margarine	*1 can (8 oz.) tomato sauce*
1 cup diced onion	*1 TBsp. vinegar*
1/2 cup diced green pepper	*4-5 dashes hot pepper sauce*
1 diced garlic clove	*1/2 tsp. salt, or to taste*
1/2 cup uncooked white rice	*1 cup cooked ham, cubed*
1 cup water	*1 cup cooked shrimp*

In a large skillet or saucepan saute onion, green pepper and garlic until tender. Add remaining ingredients except ham and shrimp, cover and simmer until rice is tender. Add ham and shrimp and simmer another three or four minutes.

❑ 1 ❑ 2 ❑ 3   854 calories

SWEET AND SOUR SHRIMP

1/2 stick margarine	1 can (8 oz.) tomato sauce
1 cup diced onion	1 can (8 oz.) pineapple bits
1 cup diced celery	1/4 cup vinegar
2 TBsp. flour	1 cup cooked shrimp

In a large skillet saute veggies until tender. Stir in flour, add remaining ingredients and stir until heated. Serve over rice.

❑ 1 ❑ 2 ❑ 3   774 calories

SHRIMP GUMBO

1/4 cup oil	1 tsp. ground bay leaf
1 cup diced onion	1 tsp. salt, or to taste
1 cup diced green pepper	4-5 dashes hot pepper sauce
1 diced garlic clove	1 can (16 oz.) crushed tomato
4 TBsp. flour	3 cups water
1 TBsp. parsley flakes	1 lb. diced ham
1/2 tsp. thyme	1 lb. cooked shrimp
1 pkg. (18 oz.) frozen okra	

In a Dutch oven saute onion, green pepper and garlic in oil until tender. Stir in flour, add remaining ingredients, bring to a boil and simmer for 10 minutes.

❑ 1 ❑ 2 ❑ 3   1,799 calories

Oyster and other boats at rest.

❧ 11 ❧

Clams

The time-honored method of consuming clams, at least in the Northwest, is to go out on a beach during a minus tide, bucket and shovel in hand, and gather whatever the law allows. They are then scrubbed and put in a bucket of water—saltwater preferred but not mandatory—and given a day for the critters to eject sand from their innards. To cook they are put in a kettle of water and the heat turned on to high. When the clam shells open, they're done. You can eat them as is, although it's customary to dip them in drawn butter or margarine.

No true clam lover discards the water used in cooking. If only a small amount of water is used, or the clams steamed instead of boiled, the juice is referred to as nectar. It may be sipped as is, or diluted to suit individual tastes. Add salt as desired, or a dab of butter. A stalk of celery added to the water at the outset yields a flavor that many people like.

The favorite steamer clam is the littleneck, either native or Manila, which are similar except for a different look to the shell. The reason they are favored is—as the name suggests—because of their little neck, the toughest part of a clam.

Butter clams, especially the smaller ones, can be eaten as steamers. The larger ones, along with cockles, horse clams (gapers), and the giant geoduck, are best ground up and used in chowders or fritters.

Eastern softshell clams are found abundantly on the Skagit River delta of Washington and in Netarts Bay in Oregon, but are scarce elsewhere. Their primary use is in fritters or chowders.

The highly prized razor clam is only found on sandy ocean beaches and may be fried, frittered or chowdered.

Unfortunately, due to their great popularity, plus red tides and pollutants affecting all clam species, digging opportunities have decreased considerably since the late Ivar Haglund strummed his guitar over the radio and warbled that he was "Surrounded by acres of clams." However, they are still available, in the shell and in cans, at seafood stores and supermarkets.

NOTE: All the following recipes use the 6 1/2-ounce can.

BASIC CLAM FRITTERS

1 beaten egg　　　　　　　　*1 can minced clams, with juice*
1/2 cup flour, or as needed　*Salt and pepper to taste*

Combine thoroughly and spoon onto a hot greased skillet.

Options: Add a tablespoon of onion soup mix, or add a few dashes of hot pepper sauce.

❑ 1 ❑ 2 ❑ 3   380 calories

CORNY CLAM FRITTERS

1 can minced clams　　*1/2 cup whole kernel corn*
4 TBsp. cornmeal　　　*1 beaten egg*
4 TBsp. biscuit mix　　*Salt and pepper to taste*

Reserve liquid from clams then combine all ingredients, adding liquid as needed for batter consistency.

❑ 1 ❑ 2 ❑ 3   610 calories

CLAM PIE

1 can minced clams with juice　*1/4 stick melted margarine*
1 cup peeled, sliced potato　　*1/2 cup biscuit mix, or as*
1 medium onion, sliced　　　　　*needed*
　　　　　　　　　　　　　　　　Salt and pepper to taste

Layer clams, potatoes and onions, and add margarine and seasonings.
Roll out biscuit mix for a pastry cover, cut into biscuits and bake 30 minutes at 400 degrees, or until crust browns.

❑ 1 ❑ 2 ❑ 3   642 calories

CLAM/CRAB CUSTARD

1 can minced clams with juice   *1 cup cooked macaroni*
1 can (6 oz.) crab   *2 beaten eggs*
1/4 stick melted margarine   *Salt and pepper to taste*

Combine all ingredients in a greased casserole dish and bake 30 minutes at 350 degrees.

❏ 1 ❏ 2 ❏ 3   565 calories

Fresh-caught chinook salmon.

❧ 12 ❧

Oysters

Oysters may be cooked in many ways, but they are also eaten raw, right out of the half shell, by true oyster lovers. Many people, it must be conceded, are repelled by the latter, although it certainly ranks as the simplest of all methods of preparing food. Much depends on the imprinting one receives as a child.

One of my earliest recollections is seeing my father open an oyster on a Puget Sound beach and downing it with obvious relish. Inevitably, I was imprinted for life.

Oysters may be consumed raw, as is, or with various sauces. Often it's a cocktail sauce, a combination of tomato sauce, chili sauce and a variety of condiments. Or, raw oysters may be eaten with just a squirt of lemon juice.

As with clams, oysters may be boiled or steamed until the shell opens, and then dipped in drawn butter or margarine. Another method is to put them on a grill over coals, or in the oven, until heat opens the shell. Take care when removing them from the grill or oven so as not to spill any of the delicious nectar hiding inside.

NOTE: Raw oysters, directly from the shell, are slippery and hard to handle when they are rolled in some type of coating for frying. A method for dealing with this is to parboil, or blanch, shucked oysters in boiling water. After the water starts boiling add the oysters, turn down the heat and leave them in the water for two or three minutes. This firms them up making them easier to handle.

FRIED OYSTERS

1 jar (10 oz.) oysters
1 beaten egg
1 TBsp. flour

Salt and pepper to taste
1/2 cup fine bread crumbs,
 or as needed

Dust blanched oysters with flour, dip in the beaten egg, roll in bread crumbs and fry in a greased skillet.

Or, combine the flour and egg and dip the oysters directly into this mixture before rolling in crumbs.

❏ 1 ❏ 2 ❏ 3   680 calories

BAKED OYSTERS

A common method is to dip blanched oysters in beaten egg and roll in seasoned cracker crumbs. You may use salt, or another seasoning as you prefer. Place them in a greased oven pan and bake 15 minutes at 400 degrees. The exact time and temperature may vary, but if you err, do it on the under-cooked side.

HANGTOWN FRY FOR THE ELITE

In the years immediately following the California gold rush of 1849, San Francisco was a rapidly growing city with many moneyed people. But, there were shortages. These included eggs and oysters, both of which commanded high prices. A popular dish among those who could afford it was Hangtown Fry, which included both items. Origin of the name is not known, but it was a pre-Hollywood demonstration of culinary conspicuous consumption.

1 jar (10 oz.) oysters
4 strips of diced bacon,
 or 1/2 stick margarine
1/2 cup diced onion
1/2 cup diced green pepper

1/2 cup diced celery
4-5 beaten eggs
1/4 cup half and half or cream
1 TBsp. Worcestershire sauce
Salt and pepper to taste

In a skillet fry the bacon, or melt margarine, and saute veggies until tender. Add the oysters, cut to desired size, and fry for a couple of minutes.

Mix the eggs, cream and seasonings, pour over the oysters and stir until the eggs are firm.

❏ 1 ❏ 2 ❏ 3   1,153 calories

HANGTOWN FRY FOR THE PEASANTS

1 jar (10 oz.) oysters
1/4 stick margarine
3-4 eggs

1/4 cup milk
1 TBsp. Worcestershire sauce
Salt and pepper to taste

Cut oysters to desired size and fry for a few minutes in the margarine. Beat remaining ingredients together, pour over the oysters and stir until the eggs are firm.

❏ 1 ❏ 2 ❏ 3   790 calories

CREAMY OYSTER BAKE

12 crushed crackers
1 jar (10 oz.) oysters
1/2 cup milk

1/2 tsp. salt, or to taste
1/4 tsp. onion salt
1/4 stick margarine

Spread half the crackers over the bottom of a greased casserole dish. Lay the oysters on the crackers, add seasonings and milk, cover with the remaining crackers, dot with margarine and bake 30 minutes at 350 degrees.

❏ 1 ❏ 2 ❏ 3   635 calories

QUICKIE OYSTER STEW

1/2 stick margarine
1/2 cup diced onion
1/2 cup diced celery, including
   leaves if desired

1 tsp. salt, or as desired
1/4 tsp. pepper
1 jar (10 oz.) oysters
1 quart milk

In a large saucepan saute onion and celery in margarine until tender. Add remaining ingredients and simmer for 10-15 minutes or until oysters are firm.

❏ 1 ❏ 2 ❏ 3   602 calories

E-Z OYSTER CHOWDER

1 jar (10 oz.) oysters
1 cup milk
1 TBsp. cornstarch

1/2 tsp. salt, or to taste
1/4 tsp. lemon pepper
1/4 stick margarine

In a saucepan combine oysters, milk and cornstarch. Add remaining ingredients, stirring under medium heat until chowder thickens and oysters become firm.

❏ 1 ❏ 2 ❏ 3   580 calories

OYSTER SOUFFLE

1/2 stick margarine	4-5 drops hot pepper sauce
2 TBsp. flour	1 jar (10 oz.) oysters
1/2 cup milk, or as needed	3 eggs, separated
Salt and pepper to taste	6 crushed crackers

Melt margarine in a skillet and stir in flour, milk and seasonings until thickened.

Remove from heat and stir in beaten egg yokes and oysters cut to desired size.

Beat egg whites stiff, fold into oyster mixture, turn into a greased casserole dish with crushed crackers on bottom, place in a pan with water and bake 30 minutes at 350 degrees.

❑ 1 ❑ 2 ❑ 3   1,060 calories

THE ULTIMATE OYSTER DISH

2 cups boiled, diced potato	2 jars (10 oz.) oysters
1/4 cup milk, or as needed	1/4 stick margarine
1/2 stick margarine	1/2 cup diced onion
3 beaten egg yolks	2 TBsp. flour
Salt and pepper to taste	1 cup oyster liquor
3 egg whites beaten stiff	1 cup half and half
1/2 cup fine dry bread crumbs	1 TBsp. parsley flakes

Boil potatoes until tender and mash them with margarine, milk, egg yolks and seasoning. Fold in stiffly beaten egg whites, sprinkle bottom of greased casserole dish with crumbs and cover with half the mashed potatoes.

In a saucepan simmer oysters in a cup of water for three minutes and remove, reserving the liquid.

In a skillet saute onion in margarine until tender. Add flour and slowly stir in oyster liquor and half and half, continuing to stir over low heat until it starts to thicken.

Combine the milk mixture with the oysters and spread over the potatoes in the casserole. Top with remaining potatoes and bake 30 minutes at 400 degrees.

❑ 1 ❑ 2 ❑ 3   2,140 calories

Oyster boats at rest in Willapa Bay, Washington.

❧ 13 ❧

Scallops

Scallops are a shellfish. But what you buy in a store bears little resemblance to such near-kin as clams and oysters. What you see is the muscle of this free-swimming mollusk.

Scallops are one of the quickest of seafoods to prepare as just 10 to 15 minutes is all the time required to cook them in a 400-degree oven.

You can also set the temperature at 350 degrees for 20 minutes, but not a bit longer because over-cooking makes them tough and rubbery. For this reason it's best not to re-heat them as leftovers. Or, if you do, use as little heat as necessary.

EASY BAKED SCALLOPS

1/2 lb. scallops	*1 TBsp. soy sauce*
1/2 cup fine, dry bread crumbs	*1 TBsp. lemon juice*
1/4 stick margarine	*Salt and pepper to taste*

Coat scallops with bread crumbs, arrange in a greased oven pan, combine soy sauce and lemon juice with melted margarine, pour over scallops and bake 15 minutes at 400 degrees.

❑ 1 ❑ 2 ❑ 3   347 calories

SCALLOPS IN HERB BUTTER

1/2 lb. scallops	*1/4 tsp. chives*
1/4 stick melted margarine	*1/4 tsp. tarragon*
1/4 tsp. onion powder	*1 TBsp. parsley flakes*
1/4 tsp. garlic powder	*1/4 tsp. salt*

Arrange scallops in a greased oven pan. Combine herbs with melted butter or margarine, pour over scallops and bake 15 minutes at 400 degrees.

❑ 1 ❑ 2 ❑ 3   385 calories

WEST COAST SEAFOOD RECIPES

SCALLOPS WITH PARSLEY

1 cup fresh bread crumbs
1/4 stick melted margarine
1/4 tsp. sage
Salt to taste

1/4 tsp. thyme
1 TBsp. parsley flakes
2 TBsp. lemon juice
1/2 lb. scallops

Combine all ingredients in a greased oven pan and bake 15 minutes at 400 degrees.

❑ 1 ❑ 2 ❑ 3   270 calories

SCALLOPS WITH MUSHROOMS

1/2 stick melted margarine
1/2 cup sliced mushrooms, or
  one 4-oz. can
1/4 cup diced green onions
1 diced garlic clove

2 TBsp. parsley flakes
1/2 lb. scallops
Salt and pepper to taste
1 cup fresh buttered bread
  crumbs

In a skillet saute mushrooms, onion and garlic in half the margarine. Stir in the parsley, scallops and seasoning, cover with bread crumbs drizzled with remaining margarine and bake 15 minutes at 400 degrees.

❑ 1 ❑ 2 ❑ 3   489 calories

SCALLOPS WITH MUSHROOMS AND PEPPERS

1/2 stick margarine
1/2 cup diced celery
1/2 cup sliced mushrooms, or
  one 4-oz. can
1/2 cup diced green peppers

2 TBsp. flour
Salt to taste
1 cup milk, or as needed
1/2 lb. scallops
1 cup fresh bread crumbs

In a skillet saute the celery, mushrooms and green peppers in half the margarine until tender. Add flour and salt, and stir in milk until thickened. Add scallops, turn into a greased casserole dish, cover with bread crumbs drizzled with remaining margarine and bake 15 minutes at 400 degrees.

❑ 1 ❑ 2 ❑ 3   670 calories

TANGY SCALLOPS

1/2 stick margarine
1 TBsp. flour
1/4 tsp. garlic powder
1 TBsp. mustard
1 tsp. prepared horseradish

1/4 tsp. celery salt
1 TBsp. lemon juice
1/2 lb. scallops
1 cup fresh buttered
  bread crumbs

In a skillet melt half the margarine. Stir in flour, adding seasonings including the lemon juice, and then stir in the scallops.

Turn into a greased casserole dish, sprinkle over with bread crumbs drizzled with the remaining margarine and bake 15 minutes at 400 degrees

❏ 1 ❏ 2 ❏ 3   475 calories

SCALLOPS WITH TOMATO AND GARLIC

2 TBsp. olive oil   *Salt and pepper to taste*
1 diced garlic clove   *1 TBsp. red wine vinegar*
1 cup diced tomatoes   *1/2 lb. scallops*

In a skillet saute garlic and tomatoes in oil until garlic is tender. Add vinegar, pour over scallops in a greased casserole dish and bake 15 minutes at 400 degrees.

❏ 1 ❏ 2 ❏ 3   265 calories

SCALLOPS AND SHRIMP

1/2 lb. scallops   *1/8 tsp. garlic powder*
1 cup cooked shrimp   *Salt and pepper to taste*
1 cup fresh bread crumbs *1/4 stick melted margarine*

Combine all ingredients in a greased oven pan or casserole dish and bake 15 minutes at 400 degrees.

❏ 1 ❏ 2 ❏ 3   570 calories

SPICY SCALLOP CHOWDER

1/2 stick margarine, or   *1/4 tsp. cayenne, or to taste*
  4 slices diced bacon   *1 TBsp. Worcestershire sauce*
1 cup diced onion   *1/2 tsp. salt, or to taste*
1 cup diced celery   *Pepper as desired*
2 TBsp. flour   *1/2 lb. scallops*
2 cups milk, or as desired *2 cups diced boiled potatoes*

Melt margarine, or fry bacon, in a deep skillet or saucepan and saute onion and celery until tender.

Add flour and slowly stir in milk until thickened. Add remaining ingredients, cover and simmer for 15-20 minutes or until scallops are tender.

NOTE: Feel free to use fewer potatoes or more scallops as you see fit.

❏ 1 ❏ 2 ❏ 3   907 calories

❧ 14 ❧

Walleye

Walleye, a freshwater fish normally associated with the northern tier states of the Midwest, are also found throughout the Columbia River system of the Northwest.

Considered by many to be the tastiest of all fish, at least those found in freshwater, there is reluctance by its admirers to use walleye in recipes that may obscure its delicate flavor.

One of the most outspoken is Wally Pease, *Outdoor Press* columnist and TV show host. In his book, *Cooking Wild*, he lists just two recipes which he considers worthy of walleye. The following are his comments, as well as his recipes:

"By far the tastiest fish in the United States is the walleyed pike. It is also more screwed up in the cooking process than you would think possible. I have seen people do things to this magnificent fish that I could hardly believe.

"Would you believe grinding up walleyes for fish balls?

"It gets worse from there on, and I can't bear to relate further atrocities. If you are of a sadistic nature go screw up a dogfish, which is pretty well screwed up to begin with, but for gosh sakes leave the poor walleye alone. The simplest methods are often best, so I will give you two very simple ways to serve walleyes. If you want to do bad things to a walleye I will not be a part of it, so two recipes are all you're going to get."

PAN FRIED WALLEYES

The first thing to do is fillet the fish, leaving completely bone-free fillets. Wash the fish quickly and gently in very cold water and set aside, then add or detract the amount of ingredients used depending on how many fillets you have to fry.

4 well beaten eggs	*Fresh ground pepper, salt*
Jane's Crazy Salt	*Butter*
Cheese crackers	*Creme sherry*
Tabasco	*Mazola*
Worcestershire sauce	*Cast iron frying pan*
Milk	*A bitty pinch of garlic*

Into a bowl combine the eggs with a dash of milk, 12 drops of Tabasco, two glurgs of Worcestershire, and a glurg or two or three of the creme sherry. Then roll out the cheese crackers until they are meal, put the meal into a large plastic or paper bag and add the salt, pepper and garlic.

Pour enough Mazola oil into the pan to nearly cover the fillets. Add a little bit of butter to this for good browning, or bacon fat for a different flavor. Soak the fillets briefly in the egg mixture, drain and then drop them into the bag. Shake until the fillets are completely covered with the meal mixture and place on a platter.

Heat the oil until a drop of water will spit, and you're ready to fry the walleyes. Try to turn only once and, when the fillets are done, place on a platter with paper toweling to absorb any excess oil. Turn and then transfer to a serving platter.

BAKED WALLEYE

I would recommend this for walleye of five pounds or more.

Scale, clean and wash the fish in cold water. Take a large flat pan or baking dish and oil it well. Cover the bottom of the pan with finely diced green onion. Put the fish on the onions and rub gently with melted butter, and then salt and pepper. Pour just enough gentle white wine to cover the bottom of the pan and cook at 400 degrees until cooked through. This should be about 10-15 minutes. Do not overcook. It may be necessary to add a bit more wine or butter, but, what the hell, live it up!

At the risk of offending Wally, here are a couple more recipes that can be used with walleye, or any other white-meated fish.

SMOKE GETS IN YOUR WALLEYES

2 TBsp. soy sauce
2 TBsp. liquid smoke
2 TBsp. oil

1/4 tsp. garlic powder
1/4 tsp. ginger
1/2 lb. walleye fillets

Combine first five ingredients, lay fillets in this marinade for a half hour or more, arrange in a greased oven pan and bake 20-25 minutes at 350 degrees.

❏ 1 ❏ 2 ❏ 3   420 calories

BAKED WALLEYE IN SOUR CREAM SAUCE

1 can (4 oz.) mushroom pieces
2 TBsp. sour cream
2 TBsp. mayonnaise

1/4 stick melted margarine
Salt and pepper to taste
1/2 lb. walleye fillets

Combine first five ingredients, spread over fillets in a greased casserole dish and bake 20-25 minutes at 350 degrees.

❏ 1 ❏ 2 ❏ 3   688 calories

❧ 15 ☙

Shad

Possibly the most under-rated fish in the Western United States is shad, both for its challenge as a gamefish and its excellence at the table. A variety of reasons may be offered.

•Shad is not commonly available in seafood markets.

•It is available to recreational anglers in a relatively few Pacific Coast rivers and, even then, for scarcely more than a month during the late spring or early summer.

•The task of cutting a boneless fillet is discouraging.

But, on the plus side, shad roe is looked upon as a delicacy, and there are liberal catch limits. They're exciting sport on light tackle and, properly prepared, are excellent table fare.

Shad, the largest member of the herring family, are broad and flat-sided, running from three to five pounds as adult spawners.

The biggest run is up the Columbia River, popular fishing places being below Bonneville Dam on both sides of the river, as well as the Washougal area, principally Camas Slough. Good runs also occur in Oregon's Umpqua and Coos rivers, and in some California streams as well.

The flesh of shad is rich in oil and is excellent smoked. There is that problem with the bones, but you can spend the time picking out bones for the next taste by savoring the flavor of the previous bite. Shad may also be pickled, or cooked in a pressure cooker and used in the same manner as tuna.

The following recipes come from the booklet, "What's So Great About Shad?" published by the former Washington Department of Fisheries, now the Department of Fish and Wildlife.

SLOW BAKED SHAD
This recipe softens the bones, as in canned salmon.

1 shad, 3 to 5-lbs.
1 tsp. salt
pepper to taste

1/4 stick melted margarine (or bacon strips as desired)
1 cup canned soup (mushroom, tomato, etc.)

Clean shad (removing the scales OK, but not necessary) and split open. Lay on a sheet of heavy-duty aluminum foil large enough to completely wrap the fish.

Season inside and out with salt and pepper, brush with melted butter or margarine, or lay strips of bacon over fish. Cover with soup.

Seal fish in foil and bake five hours at 275 degrees.

❏ 1 ❏ 2 ❏ 3

CRUSTY BAKED SHAD
Clean the fish, but leave the head and tail on.

Spray a brown paper bag with non-stick spray. To make the stuffing, chop onion and a few stalks of celery and season the combination with 1/2 tsp. salt and 1/8 tsp. pepper. Place stuffing in shad cavity and secure with skewers.

Place the fish inside the brown bag and secure it with pins or staples. Put the bag on a cookie sheet and bake for five hours at 225 degrees. Slow cooking softens the bones and the shad is a nice, crusty brown.

❏ 1 ❏ 2 ❏ 3

FRIED SHAD
Shad fillets
1-2 cups flour
Salt and pepper to taste
2 eggs

2 TBsp. water
2-3 cups cornmeal or dry bread crumbs
Shortening as needed

Put flour and cornmeal or crumbs in separate pie pans.

Beat together eggs, water and desired seasonings, roll fillets in flour and dip into egg mixture.

Coat fillets in the cornmeal or crumbs and let fillets air dry for five minutes to set coating. Fry in whatever shortening you desire.

❏ 1 ❏ 2 ❏ 3

BROILED SHAD

1 shad, 3-4 lbs.   *4 bacon strips*
1 lemon   *Salt to taste*
1 cup dry white wine

1. Clean and split the shad and place the two halves, skin side down, in a shallow glass baking dish.

2. Squeeze juice from the lemon into the wine. Lightly salt the fish, then brush the lemon juice/wine mixture over the fish and allow it to marinate for at least an hour.

3. Place fish 4 to 5 inches below oven broiler for about 15 minutes, but check no later than 10 minutes for flakiness. Do not turn fish.

❑ 1 ❑ 2 ❑ 3

Shad Roe

Roe from the female shad is considered by many to be a delicacy. Regarded on the same culinary plane as roe from sturgeon, which is processed into caviar, it is treated in a somewhat different manner. In addition to being used in hors d'oeuvres and garnishes, shad roe can also be sauteed, baked in sauce and broiled.

BASIC PREPARATION

Shad roe should be parboiled to prepare it for recipe use. But before doing so, prick the membrane with a pin to prevent the sac from bursting and scattering the tiny eggs. Place the membrane(s) in a saucepan and cover with boiling water. Simmer from three to six minutes depending on size. Drain, cool and remove the roe. It is now ready for recipe use.

SAUTEED ROE

Parboiled roe, still in the membrane, can be sauteed in a few table-spoons of butter or margarine with the addition of the seasonings of your choice. These may include, in addition to salt, chopped chives, parsley, minced shallots, tarragon, basil and etcetera. Membranes may also be dipped in egg, rolled in flour or cornmeal, and pan fried in shortening or bacon drippings.

❑ 1 ❑ 2 ❑ 3

BAKED ROE

Place parboiled roe, membrane removed, in a greased casserole dish covered with the sauce of your choice. Bake in a 375-degree oven for 15-25 minutes. Stir every five minutes.

❑ 1 ❑ 2 ❑ 3

❧ 16 ❧

Smelt

With reference to smelt in the Northwest, where they are normally available only in late winter or early spring months, it is necessary to distinguish between Columbia River smelt and surf smelt. The latter, like the grunion of California, are netted when they enter shoreline waters to spawn on gravel beaches.

However, Columbia River smelt are actually eulachons, or candlefish. The latter name results from their high oil content, much higher than surf smelt. These are the fish which inspired the British Columbia "grease trails," in which coastal Indians rendered the oil into grease and traded for goods with Indians from the interior.

The following recipes are interchangeable betwen the two, although the Columbia River "smelt" are often smoked because of their high oil content.

For purposes of simplicity a calorie count of 50 per ounce is assigned, and will be used to tally calories in the following recipes. Surf smelt would likely be closer to 30 calories per ounce, similar to rockfish. Also, a half pound of smelt is used in determining calories in the following recipes, although you needn't confine yourself to this amount. Nor do you need to weigh them as there are approximately 18 to 20 average size smelt to a pound.

PAN FRIED SMELT

1/2 lb. smelt	*1/2 tsp. salt, or to taste*
2 TBsp. cornmeal	*1/4 tsp. pepper*
1/4 cup flour	*Oil as needed for frying*

Dip smelt in milk and roll in combined cornmeal, flour and seasonings. Fry fast and hot, browning on both sides.

❏ 1   ❏ 2   ❏ 3   780 calories

BROILED SMELT

1/2 lb. smelt	1/4 stick margarine
1 TBsp. lemon juice	Salt to taste

Place smelt, salted as desired, in a greased oven pan, brush with combined margarine and lemon juice. Place 4 to 5 inches under broiling element in oven for ten minutes or so, brushing a time or two until they flake.

❏ 1 ❏ 2 ❏ 3   580 calories

OVEN-BAKED SMELT

This is a quick and low-fat way to cook smelt. Salt and pepper to taste, coat with flour or cornmeal as desired, lay in a greased oven pan and bake 20 minutes at 350 degrees.

❏ 1 ❏ 2 ❏ 3

DEEP-FRIED SMELT

2 TBsp. cornmeal	Salt and pepper to taste
1/4 cup baking mix	1/2 lb. smelt
1/2 cup milk, or as needed	1/2 cup flour, or as needed

Combine cornmeal, baking mix, milk and seasonings to make a batter. Roll smelt in flour, dip in batter and fry in hot, deep oil until browned. Drain on paper toweling.

❏ 1 ❏ 2 ❏ 3   780 calories

SMELT AU GRATIN

1/2 lb. smelt	1/2 tsp. prepared mustard
2 slices toast	1/4 tsp. paprika
1 egg	1/4 cup milk
Salt to taste	1/2 cup grated cheese

Fry smelt in oil until tender. Remove fins and bones.
Toast bread, cut each in half and lay on a greased oven pan. Cover with smelt and lay other halves of toast on top.
Combine all but the cheese together, pour over toast, sprinkle cheese over all and bake 20 minutes at 350 degrees.

❏ 1 ❏ 2 ❏ 3   805 calories

SMELT ITALIANO

1/2 lb. smelt
1/2 cup spaghetti sauce
* with mushrooms*

1/4 tsp. oregano
1/4 cup grated mozzarella
* cheese*

Arrange smelt in a greased oven pan, combine sauce and oregano, spoon over smelt, sprinkle with cheese and bake 20 minutes at 350 degrees.

❏ 1 ❏ 2 ❏ 3   630 calories

It's always nice to return home after a day of fishing

❧ 17 ❧

Squid

STIR-FRIED SQUID

1/2 lb. diced squid	1/4 cup olive oil
3 TBsp. soy sauce	1/2 tsp. ginger
1/4 tsp. pepper	1 clove minced garlic
1/4 cup dry white wine	1/2 cup sliced mushrooms
2 TBsp. cornstarch	1/4 cup diced green pepper
1/4 cup diced green onion	

Combine soy sauce, pepper, wine and cornstarch. Add diced squid and marinate while preparing remaining ingredients.

In a skillet or wok heat oil. Add remaining ingredients and stir for a couple of minutes. Add squid and continue stirring for a minute or so. Serve over hot pasta or rice.

❑ 1 ❑ 2 ❑ 3   704 calories

SQUID MARINARO

2 TBsp. olive oil	1 16-oz. can crushed tomatoes
1 minced garlic clove	1/4 tsp. oregano
1/2 cup diced onion	1/4 tsp. basil
1/2 cup chopped mushrooms	1/2 tsp. sugar
2 TBsp. flour	1/8 tsp. pepper
	1/2 lb. diced squid

In a skillet or wok heat oil and saute garlic, onion and mushrooms until tender. Add remaining ingredients, cover and simmer for about half an hour. Serve over hot pasta or rice.

❑ 1 ❑ 2 ❑ 3   582 calories

CALAMARI FRITTA

1/2 lb. squid	1/4 cup fine bread crumbs
1/2 cup flour	1/4 cup grated parmesan cheese
1/4 cup evaporated milk	Oil as needed

Combine bread crumbs and cheese. Dredge squid in flour, dip in milk, then roll in bread crumb mix. In skillet or wok fry squid until golden brown on each side, approximately 30 seconds.

❏ 1 ❏ 2 ❏ 3   700 calories

SQUID N' CHICKEN CHOWDER

1 lb. diced squid	1 cup chicken broth
1 TBsp. margarine	1 large can evaporated milk
1/2 cup diced onion	2 TBsp. margarine
1 cup diced potatoes	1 tsp. salt
1 1/2 cups water	1/4 tsp. white pepper
2 TBsp. flour	

In a large saucepan saute onion in margarine until starting to soften. Add potatoes and water, bring to a boil and simmer until potatoes are tender.

In a small bowl combine flour and chicken broth, stir until smooth, then add to potatoes and onion.

Add remaining ingredients, stirring until chowder thickens. Add squid and re-heat to short of boiling.

❏ 1 ❏ 2 ❏ 3   1,462 calories

SQUID STEW MEDITERRANEAN

1 can (16 oz.) tomatoes	1 tsp. salt
1/2 cup diced potatoes	1 bay leaf
1 cup chopped cabbage	1/4 tsp. thyme
1/2 cup diced carrots	1/4 tsp. marjoram
1/2 cup diced celery	2 TBsp. flour
1/2 cup diced onion	1/2 cup sherry
	1 lb. diced squid

Drain tomatoes, to this liquid add water to make three cups. Pour this liquid into a large saucepan.

Add the vegetables and seasonings, cover and simmer for 30 minutes, or until veggies are tender.

Add flour, squid and sherry, stirring until stew starts to thicken.

❏ 1 ❏ 2 ❏ 3   789 calories

Old painting of historic salmon cannery near Astoria, Oregon.

❧ 18 ☙

Pickled Herring

TONY FLOOR'S PICKLED HERRING

Salt well the herring you catch with medium coarse rock salt for no less than two weeks.

The following recipe is for seven or eight herring in the eight to 10-inch size. But it can be doubled, tripled, or more depending on your love of pickled herring and how many you are able to catch.

2 onions   *3 bay leaves*
1 cup water   *1 TBsp. whole black peppercorns*
4 TBsp. sugar   *1 cup vinegar*

Clean salted herring, cut off head and tail. Rinse in cold water, immerse in a mixture of half water and half milk and let stand in a cool place for six hours.

Remove and drain, cut shallow along the backbone, peel off the skin by pulling toward the tail and cut into 1-inch pieces.

Slice the onions and place alternate layers of herring and onion in a clean glass jar.

Combine remaining ingredients, boil for two or three minutes and allow to cool. When cool pour brine over herring and allow to stand two or three days in the refrigerator.

In the recipes that follow, directions are similar to the above. Simmer the vinegar and spices for 2-3 hours, then pack the herring, layered with the vegetables, in clean glass jars and let stand in a cool place for two or three days. It is recommended you prepare the brine in a non-metallic container.

These recipes will accommodate four to six pounds of herring.

PUGET SOUND PICKLED HERRING

2 cups water
1 qt. white vinegar
1 1/2 cups sugar

1/4 cup allspice
12 bay leaves
4 onions, thinly sliced
4 carrots, thinly sliced

FJORD FILLETS

1 qt. cider vinegar
1 pint white vinegar
3 cups brown sugar

3 oz. whole pickling spices
2 onions, sliced
A few red chili peppers
Bay leaves

WALLY PEASE'S PICKLING BRINE

3 pints water
1 qt. white vinegar
2 cups granulated sugar
4 cups salt

3/4 cup pickling spices
2 thinly sliced white onions,
   or more if desired
2-3 chopped garlic cloves

Wood carving of commercial salmon fisherman in South Bend, Washington.

❧ 19 ❧

Soups and Chowders

What's the difference between chowder, stew, mulligan, soup, gumbo and bouillabaise? According to the dictionary, chowder is a seafood dish, usually with a milk base. Clams are the primary piscatorial ingredient, but other types of seafood may be used.

Soups and stews normally contain some type of meat other than fish, although this is not chiseled in stone. Stews generally contain vegetables but soups may not, although it's often difficult to distinguish soup from stew. It's also difficult to differentiate between stew and mulligan.

The addition of okra transforms stew into gumbo. And when you just throw everything available into the pot and don't know what to call it, well, bouillabaise is as good a term as any.

If any of the following recipes have, in your opinion, been placed in the wrong category don't give it a thought. By whatever name there's little doubt you'll find it an excellent dish.

Although cooking for two persons is the prevailing theme of this book, and most recipes are devised for two persons with few leftovers, the very nature of creating a soup or chowder makes it difficult to rigidly adhere to this dictate. But, no problem. Save or freeze some for later use.

Chowders

SHIRLEY KANE'S SALMON CHOWDER SUPREME

1/2 stick margarine	1 can (12 oz.) evaporated milk
1/2 cup diced celery	1 can (17 oz.) creamed corn
1/2 cup diced onion	1 tsp. salt, pepper to taste
1/4 cup diced green pepper	1/2 tsp. dill
1 cup diced potato	1 minced garlic clove, or
1 cup diced carrots	1/4 tsp. garlic powder
1 can (14 1/2 oz.) chicken	1 can (15 1/2 oz.) salmon
broth	

In a deep skillet or Dutch oven saute veggies and garlic in margarine until tender. Add remaining ingredients and bring to a simmer, but do not boil.

❏ 1 ❏ 2 ❏ 3   2,097 calories

BLAINE FREER'S ULTIMATE SEAFOOD CHOWDER

I've never actually measured anything while making this chowder, but it always comes out fine. The following proportions are only suggestions to use as a guide, and to make possible a calorie count. Should you put in a little more of this, or a little less of that, it'll no doubt turn out great.

4 slices bacon, diced	1/2 lb. crab (imitation OK)
1 cup diced onion	1 can cream of potato soup
1 cup diced celery	2 cups milk (more or less)
1 cup diced potato	Salt, pepper, seafood
1 jar (10 oz.) oysters	seasoning to your taste
1 can (6 1/2 oz.) clams	3 TBsp. cornstarch
1/2 lb. shrimp	1/2 stick margarine

In a kettle or Dutch oven fry bacon. Retain fat as desired and saute onion, celery and potato until tender.

Add oysters, whole or chopped, clams, shrimp and crab.

Stir in milk and soup, adding the seasonings.

Add cornstarch, dissolved in a bit of milk, stir to just short of boiling and simmer for maybe half an hour.

❏ 1 ❏ 2 ❏ 3   2,737 calories

RITA'S RUBY CLAM CHOWDER

4 strips diced bacon
2 cups diced potato
1 cup diced onion
1 can (16 oz.) tomato sauce

2 cups chopped clams
2 cups milk
Salt, pepper, seafood
*   seasoning to taste*

In a deep saucepan fry bacon until crisp. Remove unwanted fat, saute potato and onions until tender, add remaining ingredients, bring to boil and simmer for half an hour.

If bacon fat was removed, add a quarter stick of margarine. Calorie count is based on this.

❏ 1 ❏ 2 ❏ 3   805 calories

KELLI'S KORNY KLAM CHOWDER

1 cup diced potato
1 cup diced onion
1 cup diced carrot
1 cup diced celery

1 can (4 oz.) mushroom pieces
1 can (17 oz.) creamed corn
2 cups chopped clams
2 cups milk
1/2 stick margarine

Boil veggies in a kettle until tender. Discard water, add remaining ingredients and simmer for 15-20 minutes.

❏ 1 ❏ 2 ❏ 3   805 calories

KEVIN'S CLAM CHOWDER

4 strips diced bacon
1 cup diced boiled potatoes
1 cup diced onion
1 cup minced clams

3 TBsp. flour, or as needed
2 cups milk
1/2 stick margarine
Salt and pepper to taste

In a kettle fry bacon and saute onion in bacon fat until tender. Add flour and stir in milk until blended and it starts to thicken. Add remaining ingredients and simmer for half an hour.

❏ 1 ❏ 2 ❏ 3   1,364 calories

SIMPLE SEAFOOD CHOWDER

3 cups diced potatoes   *1/2 stick margarine*
1 cup diced onion   *1 lb. cubed fillets*
2 cups milk   *Salt and pepper to taste*

In a kettle boil potatoes and onion until tender, then discard water. Add remaining ingredients, bring to short of a boil and simmer until fish flakes.

NOTE: If thickening is desired, add 2 tablespoons cornstarch dissolved in a bit of milk or water.

❑ 1 ❑ 2 ❑ 3   1,325 calories

ROCKFISH CHOWDER

1/4 stick margarine   *1 large can evaporated milk*
1 diced onion   *1 can (17 oz.) cream-style corn*
2 cups diced potatoes   *Salt and pepper to taste*
1 lb. cubed fillets

In a skillet saute onion in margarine until tender. In a kettle boil potatoes to near tender in enough water to cover. Combine all ingredients and simmer until fish flakes.

❑ 1 ❑ 2 ❑ 3   1,584 calories

SALMON/TOMATO CHOWDER

1/2 stick margarine   *2 cups milk*
1/2 cup diced onion   *1 cup tomato juice*
1/2 cup diced celery   *1 can (15 1/2 oz.) salmon*
3 TBsp. flour   *Salt and pepper to taste*

In a saucepan saute onion and celery in margarine. Stir in flour and add remaining ingredients, heating to short of boiling.

❑ 1 ❑ 2 ❑ 3   1,357 calories

Soups, Stews and Gumbos

PATSY BAKER'S MATANUSKA FISH STEW

2 TBsp. oil
2 cups diced onion
2 cloves diced garlic
1 diced green pepper
1 can (28 oz.) crushed tomatoes
3 chicken bouillon cubes
1 cup diced potatoes

1 cup dry white wine
1 cup water
1/4 tsp. thyme
1/4 tsp. basil
Salt and pepper to taste
2 lbs. fish in 1-inch cubes
1 can (7 1/2 oz.) clams

In a large kettle saute onion, garlic and green pepper in oil until tender. Add tomatoes, bouillon cubes, potatoes, wine, water and seasonings. Simmer 20 minutes.

Add cubes of fish and bring to a boil for 8-10 minutes. Add clams, including juice.

NOTE: Imitation crab may be used instead of fish.

❑ 1 ❑ 2 ❑ 3   1,483 calories

REBECCA'S FISH STEW

1/4 stick margarine
1/2 cup diced onion
1/2 cup diced green pepper
1 can (4 oz.) mushroom pieces
1 can (16 oz.) crushed tomatoes

1/4 tsp. ground bay leaf
1/4 tsp. tarragon
3-4 dashes hot pepper sauce
1/2 lb. cubed fillets
Salt and pepper to taste

In a kettle saute onion and green pepper in margarine until tender. Add other ingredients, cover, simmer until fish flakes.

❑ 1 ❑ 2 ❑ 3   582 calories

JUANITA'S FISH STEW

3 strips diced bacon
1 cup diced onion
1 tsp. paprika
1 TBsp. vinegar
1 TBsp. flour

1 cup water
1 can (8 oz.) tomato sauce
2 cups diced potatoes
Salt and pepper to taste
1 lb. cubed fillets

In a kettle fry bacon until crisp and saute onion until tender. Add paprika, vinegar, flour and water, bringing to boil. Add tomato sauce and seasonings, simmering until potatoes are tender. Add cubed fillets and simmer until fish flakes.

❑ 1 ❑ 2 ❑ 3   1,090 calories

FISH STEW FOR TWO

2 strips diced bacon	1 16-oz. can crushed tomatoes
1/2 cup diced onion	1/4 cup sherry
1/2 cup diced green pepper	Salt and pepper to taste
2 TBsp. flour	1/2 lb. cubed fillets

In a kettle or large skillet fry bacon until crisp, then saute onion and green pepper until tender. Stir in flour, then add tomatoes, sherry and seasonings. Add fillets, cover and simmer until fish flakes.

❑ 1 ❑ 2 ❑ 3   634 calories

FISH NOODLE SOUP

1 qt. water	1/4 tsp. thyme
1 cup diced carrots	Salt and pepper to taste
1 cup diced celery	1 pkg. (7 oz.) noodles or
1 cup diced onion	spaghetti
2 TBsp. parsley flakes	1 lb. cubed fillets

In a kettle boil veggies and seasonings in water and simmer for 10 minutes. Add pasta and simmer until tender. Add cubed fillets and simmer until tender.

❑ 1 ❑ 2 ❑ 3   994 calories

WARM-YOUR-INNARDS FISH STEW

1/2 stick margarine	2 cups water
1 cup diced onion	1/2 tsp. paprika
1 cup diced celery	1/2 tsp. chili powder
1 diced garlic clove	1/4 tsp. pepper
1 can (28 oz.) crushed	1 pkg. (7 oz.) spaghetti
tomatoes	1 lb. cubed fillets
1 can (8 oz.) tomato sauce	Salt to taste

In a sufficiently large kettle saute onion, celery and garlic in margarine until tender.

Add remaining ingredients except for the fillets and simmer until pasta is tender.

Add the fillets, check for needed salt, and simmer until fish flakes.

❑ 1 ❑ 2 ❑ 3   1,924 calories

TOMATO/POTATO STEW

4 strips diced bacon	2 TBsp. Worcestershire sauce
1 cup diced onion	4 TBsp. ketchup
2 cups cubed potatoes	1/2 tsp. thyme
1 can (16 oz.) crushed tomatoes	Salt and pepper to taste
1 cup water	1 lb. cubed fillets

In a large saucepan or kettle fry bacon until crisp, then saute onion and potatoes until tender.

Add remaining ingredients except fish, simmering for 20 minutes to blend flavors, then add fish and simmer until flaky.

❏ 1 ❏ 2 ❏ 3   1,244 calories

FREDERICO'S FISH STEW

1/2 stick margarine	1 qt. boiling water
1 cup diced onion	4 chicken bouillon cubes
1 cup diced celery	1 lb. cubed fillets
4 TBsp. flour	Salt and pepper to taste

In a large saucepan or kettle saute onion and celery until tender. Add flour and stir in water with dissolved bouillon until thickened, then add fillets and simmer until fish flakes.

❏ 1 ❏ 2 ❏ 3   1,024 calories

RICE AND TOMATO STEW

4 strips diced bacon	1 16-oz. can crushed tomatoes
1 cup diced onion	1/2 cup uncooked instant rice
1 cup diced celery	1 lb. cubed fillets
2 cups water	Salt and pepper to taste

In a large saucepan or kettle fry bacon until crisp, then saute onion and celery until tender.

Add water, tomato and rice, stirring until rice is done.

Add fillets, check for seasoning, and simmer until fish flakes.

❏ 1 ❏ 2 ❏ 3   1,164 calories

SIMPLE SALMON BISQUE

1 can (7 3/4 oz.) salmon	1/4 tsp. onion powder
1 can cond. green pea soup	2 cups milk
1 can cond. cream of celery soup	1 cup croutons

Combine first five ingredients in a saucepan and heat to just short of boiling. Serve with croutons.

❏ 1 ❏ 2 ❏ 3   1,150 calories

SALMON/TOMATO STEW

1/4 stick margarine	*1 can (15 1/2 oz.) salmon*
1/2 cup diced onion	*1 can (16 oz.) crushed tomatoes*
1/2 cup diced green pepper	*1 can whole kernel corn*
	Salt and pepper to taste

In a large saucepan or kettle saute veggies in margarine until tender. Add remaining ingredients and simmer 15-20 minutes.

❏ 1 ❏ 2 ❏ 3   1,234 calories

SUSAN'S SALMON STEW

4 strips diced bacon	*1 16-oz. can crushed tomatoes*
1 cup diced onion	*1 can (8 oz.) tomato sauce*
1/2 cup diced green pepper	*2 cups chicken bouillon*
1/2 cup diced celery	*1 can (15 1/2 oz.) salmon*
1 can (4 oz.) mushroom pieces	*Salt and pepper to taste*

In a large saucepan or kettle fry bacon until crisp, then saute onion, green pepper and celery until tender. Add remaining ingredients but taste before adding further seasonings. Simmer 15-20 minutes.

❏ 1 ❏ 2 ❏ 3   1,249 calories

SHRIMP CREOLE SOUP

2 TBsp. oil	*1 cup water*
1/2 cup diced celery	*1/4 tsp. ground bay leaf*
1/2 cup diced green pepper	*1/4 tsp. thyme*
1 minced garlic clove	*1/4 tsp. white pepper*
1 pkg. chicken-rice soup mix	*3-4 dashes hot pepper sauce*
1 16-oz. can crushed tomatoes	*1/4 tsp. white pepper*
1 can (8 oz.) tomato sauce	*1/2 lb. shrimp*

In a kettle saute veggies until tender. Add ingredients all but shrimp, simmer 10 minutes, add shrimp and simmer another 10 minutes.

❏ 1 ❏ 2 ❏ 3   592 calories

SHELL N' FINFISH STEW

4 strips diced bacon
1 cup diced onion
1/2 tsp. thyme
1/2 tsp. basil
1/2 tsp. oregano
1/4 tsp. ground bay leaves

1 cup water
1/2 cup dry white wine
2 TBsp. cornstarch
1/2 lb. cubed fillets
1 can (6 1/2 oz.) minced clams
Salt and pepper to taste

In a kettle or Dutch oven fry bacon until crisp, saute onion until tender. Add herbs and water, bring to a boil and stir in cornstarch dissolved in a bit of water.

Add fillets and clams, season to taste, cover and simmer until fish flakes.

❏ 1 ❏ 2 ❏ 3   844 calories

WILLAPA BAY BOWL
(Reprinted from "The Intermediate Eater")

1/4 stick margarine
1 clove garlic, minced
1/2 cup diced green onion
2 TBsp. flour
3 cups chicken bouillon

1 can (14 oz.) artichoke
  hearts, drained
1/2 tsp. red pepper
1/4 tsp. anise seed
2 jars (10 oz.) small oysters
Salt and pepper to taste

In a saucepan saute garlic and green onion until tender. Add flour and stir in bouillon until thickened.

Add artichokes and seasonings, simmering for a few minutes. Add oysters, simmering until they are firm.

❏ 1 ❏ 2 ❏ 3   807 calories

OLE'S OYSTER STEW

1/2 stick margarine
1 cup diced onion
1 cup diced celery
1 cup diced potato

2 cups milk
1 jar (10 oz.) oysters
2 TBsp. cornstarch (optional)
Salt and pepper to taste

In a saucepan saute veggies in margarine until tender. Add milk, oysters and seasonings, simmering until oysters are firm. If thicker stew desired, add cornstarch dissolved in milk.

❏ 1 ❏ 2 ❏ 3   1,024 calories

Bouillabaise

Although the name is French, bouillabaise has an indeterminate, although primarily Mediterannean, origin. An amalgam of seafood, vegetables and spices assembled by fishermen, there is no single recipe. The common bond is that it be highly spiced and contain two or more types of seafood. Obviously, an imaginative cook can devise his or her own recipe.

In the Old Country bouillabaise was made using the whole fish, not fillets or cans purchased from the supermarket. If you want to go the old-fashioned way, here's how:

1. Fillet the fish, cut the fillets into cubes and set aside.

2. Boil all of what remains—head, fins, entrails, skin—in a quart of water, or enough to cover, for a half hour or so. Strain to obtain a clear fish stock and discard the rest. Use the stock instead of plain water in the following recipes.

BORSETH'S BOUILLABAISE

1/2 stick margarine	*1/4 tsp. thyme*
1 cup diced onion	*1/4 tsp. ground bay leaf*
1 cup diced celery	*1/2 lb. shrimp*
1 diced garlic clove	*1 can (10 oz.) oysters*
1 16-oz. can crushed tomatoes	*1 lb. cubed fillets*
2 cups fish stock or water	*Salt and pepper to taste*

In a kettle or Dutch oven saute onion, celery and garlic in margarine until tender. Add remaining ingredients, bring to a boil, cover and simmer until fish flakes.

NOTE: A suggestion would be to sprinkle parmesan cheese on bread, toast it in the oven, place a slice in a bowl and cover it with bouillabaise.

❏ 1 ❏ 2 ❏ 3   1,554 calories

SEMRAU'S SIMPLE BOUILLABAISE

1/2 stick margarine	*1 16-oz. can crushed tomatoes*
1 cup diced onion	*2 cups fish stock or water*
2 TBsp. Worcestershire sauce	*1 cup dry red wine*
1/2 tsp. garlic powder	*1/2 lb. shrimp*
1/2 tsp. ground bay leaf	*1 can (10 oz.) clams*
1/2 tsp. black pepper	*1 lb. cubed fillets*
	Salt to taste

In a kettle or Dutch oven saute onion until tender. Add remaining ingredients, cover and simmer until fish flakes.

❏ 1 ❏ 2 ❏ 3   1,497 calories

BOUILLABAISE PIE

1/2 stick margarine
4 TBsp. flour
2 cups fish stock or
   chicken bouillon
1 pkg. (10 oz.) frozen peas,
   or a 17-oz. can, drained
1 cup boiled diced potatoes

1 cup cooked shrimp
1 can (6 1/2 oz.) tuna
1/2 lb. cubed fillets
Salt and pepper to taste
1/2 cup baking mix, or as needed
   to make a crust

In a skillet stir flour into melted margarine, add fish stock or bouillon, stirring until thickened.

Combine remaining ingredients in a greased casserole dish, cover with biscuit dough and bake 30 minutes at 400 degrees.

❏ 1 ❏ 2 ❏ 3   1,560 calories

PETERSON'S BOUILLABAISE DELUXE

1/2 stick margarine
1 cup diced onion
1 cup diced celery
1 diced garlic clove
3 TBsp. flour
1 qt. fish stock or water
1 cup dry white wine
1 can (16 oz.) crushed tomato
2 TBsp. parsley flakes

2 TBsp. lemon juice
1/4 tsp. ground bay leaf
1/4 tsp. saffron
1/4 tsp. cayenne pepper
1 tsp. salt, or to taste
1/2 lb. shrimp
1 jar (10 oz.) oysters
1 can (6 oz.) crab
1 lb. cubed fillets

In a kettle or Dutch oven saute onion, celery and garlic in margarine until tender. Stir in flour, then add remaining ingredients except seafood. Bring to a boil and simmer 20 minutes to blend flavors.

Add seafood and continue simmering until fish flakes.

❏ 1 ❏ 2 ❏ 3   1,854 calories

SHRIMP GUMBO

1/4 cup oil
1 cup diced onion
1 cup diced green pepper
1 diced garlic clove
4 TBsp. flour
1 TBsp. parsley flakes
1/2 tsp. thyme
1 pkg. (18 oz.) frozen okra

1 tsp. ground bay leaf
1 tsp. salt, or to taste
4-5 dashes hot pepper sauce
1 can (16 oz.) crushed tomato
3 cups water
1 lb. diced ham
1 lb. shrimp

In a Dutch oven saute onion, green pepper and garlic in oil until tender. Stir in flour, add remaining ingredients, bring to a boil and simmer for 10 minutes.

❏ 1 ❏ 2 ❏ 3   1,799 calories

⁑ 20 ⁑

From the Smoker

Most any kind of seafood can be smoked. However, among fish from saltwater, oilier species such as salmon and sablefish, or black cod, are preferred. And among salmon, coho and Chinook, especially spring Chinook, are considered superior. From lakes and rivers lake trout (also called mackinaw and char), kokanee, Columbia River smelt and sturgeon are stars of the smoker. Trout, especially those larger than pan-sized, can also be smoked with excellent results.

Oysters and clams are most often cooked in more traditional ways, but they also can be smoked with good results.

Possibly the single most important factor in producing superior results from your smoker is to use fresh, superior fish.

Large wooden smokers have been built by hand, and others from discarded refrigerators. However, in an increasingly urbanized world it's safe to say that most home smoking is done with an electric smoker.

The seafood may be smoked with either a hot or a cold smoke. In a cold smoke the fire is a distance away from the smoker itself and the smoke is directed to the fish through a tunnel or some type of conduit. The fish, then, is cured strictly by the smoke and takes considerably longer—like days, perhaps—than with a hot smoke to effect a cure.

In the 1940s my father, a Camano Island resident, cold-smoked the salmon he caught. World War II's General Mark Clark, for awhile a Camano resident and neighbor, declared it the greatest smoked salmon he'd ever tasted.

A hot smoke is what you get from an electric smoker, in which both heat and smoke do the job.

Any hardwood may be used, such as alder, maple, apple and hickory. In an electric smoker the wood used is in the form of sawdust or chips and may be obtained from a variety of sources, including sporting goods stores, that sell smokers.

In addition to fresh fish, a good smoked product results from proper preparation and a brine to your taste. Different brines result in different tastes, and following are some suggestions. Rock salt is commonly used, but non-iodized salt from the grocery store works equally well. Do NOT used iodized salt as it may leave a bitter taste.

The following directions are pretty much standard for all brines:
•Always use a glass or plastic container. Do NOT use aluminum as the salt may react to the metal.
•Six to eight hours in the brine will usually suffice. The fish will absorb just so much brine and no more.
•After removing fish from the brine, pat dry with toweling and let dry for a couple of hours, or overnight.
•If you are using a simple brine you might want to easily fancy it up a bit by sprinkling on such seasonings as garlic or onion salt, black pepper, dill, or whatever else you wish, before smoking.
•If you used granulated sugar in the brine you might dissolve some brown sugar in water and brush the fish before smoking.
•By rule of thumb, six to eight hours is sufficient for a medium smoke in an electric smoker, not too soft yet not so hard as Alaska squaw candy.
•Three or four pans of wood chips or sawdust should suffice, as with brine, the fish will only absorb just so much smoke.

Brines for Salmon and Other Fish

SIMPLE BRINE

1 quart water	1/2 cup brown sugar
1/2 cup non-iodized salt	1/4 cup soy sauce (optional)

For a milder taste you might try 1/3 salt to 2/3 brown sugar.

❏ 1 ❏ 2 ❏ 3

FANCY BRINE

1 quart water	1/4 tsp. pepper
1/2 cup brown sugar	1/4 tsp. hot pepper sauce
1/2 cup rock salt	1/2 cup dry white wine
1/2 tsp. garlic salt	1/2 cup soy sauce

❏ 1 ❏ 2 ❏ 3

FANCIER BRINE

1 quart water
1/2 cup rock salt
1/2 cup white sugar
1/4 cup rum
1/4 cup lemon juice

3 cloves crushed garlic
3 TBsp. pickling spices
1/4 tsp. lemon-pepper
3 bay leaves

❏ 1 ❏ 2 ❏ 3

FRED TEENY'S BRINE

The following recipe appeared in *The Outdoor Press*, Spokane, Washington. Fred Teeny was the father of Jim Teeny, originator of the Teeny Nymph and other steelhead and trout flies.

5 cups luke warm water
3/4 cup rock salt

3/4 cup brown sugar

After brining and drying the fillets, mix a cup of brown sugar in a bag with one tablespoon each of onion and garlic powder. Shake fillets in the bag and lay them on the grills, larger pieces on the bottom, smaller on top. Use four pans of chips, 1 1/2 to 2 hours for each pan. When top pieces are done, all are done.

NOTE: Add a cup of dark rum to the brine for a more robust flavor.

❏ 1 ❏ 2 ❏ 3

DRY BRINE

Mix 1/4 cup each garlic and onion powder, plus one cup sugar. Shake brine and fish together in a brown or plastic bag.

❏ 1 ❏ 2 ❏ 3

Brine for Trout and Other Seafood

The first fish we ever smoked were from a (then) remote lake in British Columbia. We simply split the fish open and rubbed on salt and brown sugar. It's a simple but effective method. If you want a gourmet treat, though, try the following:

SAM COVINGTON'S SMOKED TROUT

1 quart of water
1/2 cup rock salt
1 TBsp. Worcestershire sauce

1 TBsp. Johnny's Seafood
seasoning
1 tsp. hot pepper sauce

According to Sam Covington, a resident of Mar-Don Resort on Potholes Reservoir near Moses Lake, Washington, after cleaning, the fish should be left in the brine about 12 hours and should go through two "smokes" of about two hours each.

❑ 1 ❑ 2 ❑ 3

SMOKY SMELT

1/2 cup non-iodized salt
1/2 cup brown sugar
1/4 cup soy sauce
1/4 cup wine vinegar
1 TBsp. Worcestershire sauce

1 tsp. paprika
1 tsp. chili powder
1 tsp. garlic powder
1/4 tsp. pepper
6 cups warm water

This is enough brine for many pounds of smelt, and will do for other types of fish as well

❑ 1 ❑ 2 ❑ 3

SMOKED OYSTERS

After shucking, blanch the oysters in hot water for two or three minutes to firm them up. If you don't have a shucking knife, oysters can be opened by steaming, boiling or baking, which also firms them up.

Soak them in a simple brine for an hour or so. You needn't use a fancy brine with exotic herbs and spices as the oyster's dominant flavor will take command in any event.

After removing from the brine, let them air dry for an hour or so, or pat dry with a towel as you do with fish. If the oysters are so small they fall through the grill, place them on an oiled screen or cheesecloth.

The smoking time is variable according to your taste. So, take one out after an hour and sample it, then do so every hour until they've acquired the perfection you're seeking.

❑ 1 ❑ 2 ❑ 3

SMOKED CLAMS

Instructions for smoking clams are identical to oysters when the clams are opened by steaming or boiling. Littlenecks and butter clams are recommended for smoking. Horse clams and cockles are OK if you REALLY want to give your jaws a workout.

❑ 1   ❑ 2   ❑ 3

SMOKED CRAYFISH, PRAWNS AND SHRIMP

Pre-cook and peel, then follow brining and smoking directions as for oysters and clams.

❑ 1   ❑ 2   ❑ 3

❧ 21 ❧

Sauces and Poaching Liquids

Sauces

Adding sauce to fish may make all the difference between an ordinary dish and a delightful repast. As with the infinite methods of preparing fish, the variety of sauces that may be devised by imagina tive chefs is beyond calculation. This chapter just scratches the surface.

NOTE: Sour cream is called for in many sauce recipes. However, you can use sour cream substitutes such as plain yogurt or Imo with little change in taste.

MAYONNAISE AND . . .

A tasty sauce to put over a fish fillet needn't be a big production. Mayonnaise, that ubiquitous presence in so many seafood recipes, can serve the purpose with no further help, especially with salmon and cracked crab.

However, the addition of a dollop of this, or a spoonful of that, can give it an entirely different character. For example, to a half cup of mayonnaise add a tablespoon of dill pickle juice, or horseradish, or ketchup, or tomato paste, or whatever else you may decide upon.

TARTAR SAUCE

A popular sauce with fish, tartar sauce is basically mayonnaise with the addition of a variety of ingredients beyond those mentioned in the preceding paragraph. Many excellent commercial brands are available, but if you'd like to craft your own, following are some suggestions with the simplest of directions—just mix all the ingredients together.

QUICK BUT TASTY TARTAR

4 TBsp. mayonnaise	*1 TBsp. parsley flakes*
3 TBsp. finely diced onion	*2 TBsp. lemon juice*
2 TBsp. finely diced dill pickle	

❑ 1 ❑ 2 ❑ 3   404 calories

SWEET BUT SPICY TARTAR

4 TBsp. mayonnaise	*2 TBsp. diced green onion*
2 TBsp. diced sweet pickle	*1/2 tsp. tarragon*
1 TBsp. parsley flakes	*1 tsp. prepared mustard*

❑ 1 ❑ 2 ❑ 3   415 calories

TARTAR SAUCE WITH SOUR CREAM

2 TBsp. mayonnaise	*2 TBsp. finely diced onion*
2 TBsp. sour cream	*2 TBsp. lemon juice*
2 TBsp. diced sweet pickle	*Salt to taste*

❑ 1 ❑ 2 ❑ 3   291 calories

BASIC WHITE SAUCE

Melt 1/2 stick of butter or margarine in a saucepan or double boiler, add two tablespoons of flour and stir until melted and blended. Stir in milk to desired thickness and add salt and pepper to taste. NOTE: If you have fish stock on hand use it instead of milk.

To the basic white sauce a variety of other ingredients may be added such as a tablespoon of ketchup or mustard. Or, you can really give it body by adding sliced hard-boiled egg, grated cheese, a can of shrimp, crab, tuna, or any combination of the preceding.

ART HAUGE'S SEAFOOD SAUCE

Here is a simple, but versatile sauce that can be used in a crab or shrimp cocktail, with fish, cracked crab, or any type of seafood. Just three ingredients are used—ketchup, horseradish and lemon—the proportions dictating the final result. You may use horseradish strong enough to make your eyes water, horseradish sauce or a milder whippped or cream-style. A suggestion would be to mix the following and, if your taste buds agree, increase the recipe to whatever amount you desire.

1/2 cup ketchup	*1 heaping teaspoon cream-style*
1 TBsp. lemon juice	*horseradish*

❑ 1 ❑ 2 ❑ 3   291 calories

LEMON SAUCE

1/4 stick margarine
2 TBsp. flour
Salt to taste
1/4 tsp. dry mustard

1 cup milk, or as needed
2 TBsp. lemon juice
1 tsp. grated lemon peel
  (optional)

In a saucepan over low heat stir together flour and margarine, adding salt and mustard. Stir in milk until thickened. Remove from heat and stir in lemon juice and lemon peel.

❑ 1 ❑ 2 ❑ 3   295 calories

LEMON/SOUR CREAM SAUCE

1/2 cup sour cream
2 TBsp. diced green onion,
  with tops

2 TBsp. lemon juice
1 tsp. sugar
4-5 dashes hot pepper sauce

❑ 1 ❑ 2 ❑ 3   257 calories

LEMON/PARSLEY SAUCE

3/4 cup water
1 TBsp. cornstarch
1 TBsp. lemon juice
1 TBsp. grated lemon peel

1/2 tsp. sugar
1/4 tsp. salt
1 TBsp. parsley flakes
1/8 stick margarine

Dissolve cornstarch in water and combine in a saucepan over medium heat with lemon juice and grated peel, sugar and salt, stirring until thickened. Add parsley and margarine, stirring until margarine has melted.

❑ 1 ❑ 2 ❑ 3   122 calories

MUSTARD HOT SAUCE

1 beaten egg
1 tsp. prepared mustard
1 TBsp. onion flakes

1 TBsp. wine vinegar
1/2 cup sour cream
Dash cayenne

Combine ingredients and heat in saucean until thickened.

❑ 1 ❑ 2 ❑ 3   320 calories

MUSTARD SWEET SAUCE

1 TBsp. flour	2 beaten eggs
1 TBsp. dry mustard	3/4 cup milk
1 TBsp. sugar	1/4 cup white vinegar
1/2 tsp. salt	Pepper to taste

In a bowl mix first four ingredients. Beat eggs, add to dry ingredients and stir in milk.

Pour into a double boiler, heating and stirring until thickened. Add vinegar and pepper, heating but not boiling.

❏ 1 ❏ 2 ❏ 3   343 calories

MUSTARD SAUCE WITH MUSHROOMS

1 cup diced onion	1 can (4 oz.) mushroom pieces
1/4 stick margarine	2 TBsp. sour cream
1 TBsp. flour	1/2 tsp. dry mustard
1/2 cup milk, or as needed	Salt and pepper to taste

In a skillet saute onion in margarine until tender. Add flour and stir in milk until thickened. Add remaining ingredients, stirring until re-heated.

❏ 1 ❏ 2 ❏ 3   334 calories

DIJON CREAM SAUCE

1/2 cup finely diced onion	1 cup milk
1/4 stick margarine	1 TBsp. Dijon mustard
1 TBsp. flour	Salt and pepper to taste

In a saucepan saute onion in margarine until tender. Add flour, stirring in milk until thickened, then add mustard and seasonings.

❏ 1 ❏ 2 ❏ 3   367 calories

DIJON SAUCE WITH MUSHROOMS

1/4 stick margarine	1/4 cup dry white wine
1/4 tsp. garlic powder, or	1 TBsp. Dijon mustard
1 diced garlic clove	1 TBsp. cornstarch
1 can (4 oz.) mushroom pieces	1 TBsp. lemon juice
1/2 cup milk, or half and half	Salt and pepper to taste

In a skillet melt margarine and add remaining ingredients except lemon juice and seasonings, stirring until thickened. Add lemon juice and season to taste.

❏ 1 ❏ 2 ❏ 3   298 calories

SHERRY SAUCE

1 TBsp, flour	1/4 cup salad oil
1 egg, separated	1/4 cup sour cream
1/2 tsp. dry mustard	Salt and pepper to taste
1/2 cup sherry	

Combine flour, egg yoke, mustard and sherry in a double boiler, heat, stirring until thickened.

Add beaten egg white, oil, sour cream and seasonings to taste, stirring until egg whites are thoroughly mixed.

❏ 1 ❏ 2 ❏ 3   805 calories

MUSHROOM SAUCE WITH SHERRY

1/4 stick margarine	1 can (4 oz.) mushroom pieces
1 TBsp. flour	1/4 cup sherry
1/4 cup sour cream	Salt and pepper to taste

In a saucepan melt margarine and stir in remaining ingredients.

❏ 1 ❏ 2 ❏ 3   523 calories

SIMPLE CREAM AND LEMON SAUCE

1/4 stick margarine	1/2 cup sour cream
1 TBsp. flour	1 TBsp. lemon juice
	Salt and pepper to taste

In a saucepan melt margarine and stir in remaining ingredients.

❏ 1 ❏ 2 ❏ 3   445 calories

FANCY WINE SAUCE

1/4 stick margarine	1/4 tsp. marjoram
1/4 cup diced onion	1/4 tsp. thyme
1/4 cup diced celery	1/3 cup milk
1 TBsp. flour	1/2 cup grated cheese
Salt and pepper to taste	1/4 cup dry white wine

In a saucepan saute onion and celery until tender.

Add flour and seasonings, stirring in milk until thickened.

Stir in cheese until melted, remove from heat and slowly blend in wine.

❏ 1 ❏ 2 ❏ 3   451 calories

LUE PARK'S DILL/SOUR CREAM SAUCE

1 TBsp. margarine　　　　　*1/2 cup milk*
1 TBsp. finely diced onion　*1 TBsp. grated parmesan*
1 TBsp. flour　　　　　　　*1/2 cup sour cream*
1/2 tsp. paprika　　　　　　*1 beaten egg*
1/4 tsp. dill　　　　　　　　*Salt to taste*

In a saucepan saute onion in margarine until tender. Add flour, paprika and dill, stirring in milk until thickened, then blend in cheese.

Combine sour cream and egg and stir into sauce over low heat until blended and hot, but do not boil. Add salt to taste.

NOTE: For a greater amount you may use a cup of sour cream, although two tablespoons of parmesan cheese will still be OK.

❏ 1　❏ 2　❏ 3　　560 calories

SOUR CREAM/HORSERADISH SAUCE

1/2 cup sour cream　　*2 TBsp. finely diced onion*
2 tsp. horseradish　　*Salt and pepper to taste*
1/2 tsp. dill weed

❏ 1　❏ 2　❏ 3　　250 calories

QUICK N' SIMPLE CLAM SAUCE

1/4 stick margarine　　　　*1 can (6 oz.) minced clams*
1 TBsp. flour　　　　　　　*Salt to taste*
1/2 cup milk, or as needed　*Dash of lemon pepper*

In a skillet melt margarine and add remaining ingredients, including clam juice, stirring until thickened.

❏ 1　❏ 2　❏ 3　　395 calories

FOO YUNG SAUCE

1 cup chicken bouillon　*1 TBsp. sugar*
1 TBsp. soy sauce　　　*1 TBsp. cornstarch*

In a skillet combine first three ingredients, then stir in cornstarch, dissolved in a bit of water, until thickened.

❏ 1　❏ 2　❏ 3　　65 calories

SWEET AND SOUR SAUCE

1/4 cup water	*1/2 cup chopped tomatoes*
1/4 cup red wine vinegar	*1/4 cup finely diced onion*
1 TBsp. sugar	*1 TBsp. cornstarch*
2 TBsp. soy sauce	*1/4 cup water*

In a saucepan combine water, vinegar, sugar, soy sauce, tomato and onion. Simmer 10 minutes, dissolve cornstarch in water and stir into sauce until thickened.

❏ 1 ❏ 2 ❏ 3   113 calories

SIMPLE HOLLANDAISE SAUCE

1/2 stick margarine	*1 TBsp. lemon juice, or to taste*
3 egg yokes	*2 TBsp. water, or as needed*

Place margarine, egg yokes and lemon juice in a cold saucepan and heat, stirring until sauce thickens. If sauce appears too thick, add hot water as needed, then salt to taste.

❏ 1 ❏ 2 ❏ 3   540 calories

Poaching Liquids

Poaching liquids, or court bouillon, and sauce go hand-in-hand with poached fish, which generally requires a sauce to create a dish that will delight the palate.

The simplest of poaching liquids is plain water, perhaps with the addition of salt, and is almost certainly used with a sauce in mind. But more sophisticated poaching liquids, called court bouillon, can inject a flavor of their own into the fish from the vegetables, herbs and spices they contain.

A step beyond court bouillon is fish stock in which the unused portion of a filleted fish—the head, skin, fins and tail—is boiled in water, or in a previously made court bouillon. If you have no unused portions of a fish on hand you may create a fish stock by saving the court bouillon in which you have previously poached a fish. Some of the flavor of that fish will enhance the flavor already in the bouillon, which can be frozen and used again.

A final step, for those willing to go that extra mile, is to continue boiling the fish stock down to a concentrate embodying the very essence of the flavor it contains, and which is used in making various sauces.

Fish may be poached whole or in fillets, although in whatever form care must be taken to lift the fish from the poaching liquid without it falling apart. Poaching kettles for fish are made in various sizes. However, without a kettle designed for poaching fish, laying it on cheesecloth will do the trick.

When poaching, never bring the liquid to a rolling boil. Simmer, and then only for a few minutes depending on the thickness of the fish or fillets. By rule of thumb, allow 8 to 10 minutes per inch of thickness.

QUICK COURT BOUILLON

2 cups water	*1/2 tsp. salt*
2 cups sherry, or other	*1/2 tsp. pepper*
dry white wine	*1 sliced lemon*

❑ 1 ❑ 2 ❑ 3

SIMPLE COURT BOUILLON

3 cups water	*1/2 tsp. salt*
1 sliced onion	*1/2 tsp. pepper*
1/4 cup vinegar	*1 bay leaf*
1 tsp. Worcestershire sauce	*1/4 tsp. thyme*

❑ 1 ❑ 2 ❑ 3

COURT BOUILLON WITH VEGGIES

1 quart of water	*1 sliced lemon*
1/2 cup diced carrots	*1/4 cup wine vinegar*
1/2 cup diced onion	*1 tsp. salt*
1/2 cup diced celery	*1/4 tsp. ground cloves*

❑ 1 ❑ 2 ❑ 3

WITH VEGGIES AND WINE

2 cups water	*2 cups dry white wine*
1/2 cup diced onion	*2 TBsp. white vinegar*
1/2 cup diced carrot	*1 TBsp. salt*
1/2 cup diced celery	*5 peppercorns*
2 TBsp. parsley flakes	*1 bay leaf*

❑ 1 ❑ 2 ❑ 3

Charles Amato displays a fine chinook salmon.

❧ 22 ☙

Salads

One normally associates salad and seafood with tuna or shrimp in a tossed salad. There are, however, numerous other ways in which versatile seafood can be used in a salad by adventuresome kitchen mechanics. Following are just a few examples.

NOTE: Unless otherwise specified, directions are the same for all recipes. Combine ingredients and serve with tomato, lettuce and hard-boiled egg slices as desired.

Salmon

SIMPLE CELERY SALAD

1 can (7 3/4 oz.) salmon	1/4 cup finely diced celery
2 TBsp. mayonnaise	1/4 cup finely diced onion
1 TBsp. lemon juice	4-5 dishes hot pepper sauce
	Salt and pepper to taste

❑ 1 ❑ 2 ❑ 3   522 calories

SALMON/EGG SALAD

1 can (7 3/4 oz.) salmon	2 TBsp. finely diced onion
2 hard-boiled eggs, chopped	2 TBsp. mayonnaise
2 TBsp. diced green pepper	2 TBsp. lemon juice
	Salt and pepper to taste

❑ 1 ❑ 2 ❑ 3   684 calories

SALMON/POTATO SALAD

1 can (7 3/4 oz.) salmon	2 TBsp. mayonnaise
1 cup cooked, diced potato	2 TBsp. lemon juice
1/4 cup diced green onion	Salt and pepper to taste

❑ 1 ❑ 2 ❑ 3   601 calories

CREAMY SALMON

1 can (7 3/4 oz.) salmon
2 hard-boiled eggs, chopped
2 TBsp. parsley flakes
1/4 cup finely diced celery
1/4 cup finely diced onion

2 TBsp. lemon juice
3 TBsp. sour cream
1/4 tsp. dill weed
Salt and pepper to taste

❑ 1 ❑ 2 ❑ 3   595 calories

With Tuna

QUICK TUNA LUNCH

1 can (6 1/2 oz.) tuna
1 cup chopped lettuce
1/2 cup diced celery
1/2 cup diced zucchini or
  cucumber

1 TBsp. vinegar
2 TBsp. lemon juice
1 TBsp. mayonnaise
Salt and pepper to taste

❑ 1 ❑ 2 ❑ 3   340 calories

TUNA AND RICE SALAD

1 can (6 1/2 oz.) tuna
1 cup cold cooked rice
1/4 cup Italian dressing
1/4 cup diced celery

1/4 cup diced green onion
1/4 cup diced green pepper
  (optional)
Salt and pepper to taste

❑ 1 ❑ 2 ❑ 3   542 calories

TUNA/SOUR CREAM SALAD

1 can (6 1/2 oz.) tuna
3 TBsp. sour cream
2 TBsp. lemon juice
1/4 cup diced green pepper

1/4 cup diced onion
Dash of onion powder
Salt and pepper to taste

❑ 1 ❑ 2 ❑ 3   320 calories

TUNA WALDORF SALAD

1 can (6 1/2 oz.) tuna
2 TBsp. lemon juice
2 cups diced apple
1/2 cup finely diced celery

1/2 cup raisins
4 TBsp. mayonnaise
1/4 cup chopped walnuts

Flake tuna and drizzle lemon juice over apple. Combine with celery, raisins and mayonnaise and top each serving with walnuts.

❑ 1 ❑ 2 ❑ 3   1,185 calories

In Molds with Gelatin

SALMON/TOMATO MOLD

1 cup hot water
2 envelopes plain gelatin
1 can (8 oz.) tomato sauce
4 TBsp. sour cream
1 can (7 3/4 oz.) salmon

3-4 drops hot pepper sauce
1/2 cup diced celery
1/2 cup diced green pepper
1/2 cup diced onion

In saucepan add gelatin to water and heat until dissolved.
Blend in tomato sauce, sour cream, salmon and hot pepper sauce, and chill until partially set in an hour or so.

Stir in celery, green pepper and onion so they are evenly distributed and pour into individual greased molds, or a single larger mold. Serve with lettuce, tomatoes or hard-boiled eggs.

❑ 1 ❑ 2 ❑ 3   544 calories

FANCY SHRIMP MOLD

1 pkg. lime or lemon Jello
1 cup hot water
4 TBsp. sour cream

1/4 cup whipping cream
1 cup cooked shrimp
1/2 cup finely diced celery
1 jar (3 oz.) stuffed olives

In a large saucepan dissolve Jello in hot water. Add sour cream and blend well, using an eggbeater if necessary. Put in the refrigerator to chill.

When it starts to thicken—in about an hour or a little more—fold in whipping cream beaten stiff, stir in remaining ingredients and spoon into individual greased molds, or a single larger mold. Serve with lettuce, tomatoes or hard-boiled eggs.

❑ 1 ❑ 2 ❑ 3   600 calories

TUNA/MUSHROOM MOLD

1 can cream of mushroom soup
1 pkg. unflavored gelatin
1 pkg. (3 oz.) cream cheese
1 can (6 1/2 oz.) tuna
1/2 cup grated carrot

1/2 cup finely diced celery
1/4 cup diced green onion
2 TBsp. parsley flakes
3 TBsp. lemon juice
4-5 dashes hot pepper sauce

Add gelatin, dissolved in 1/4 cup of water, and cream cheese to hot soup, stirring until blended.

Lower heat, stir in remaining ingredients and spoon into well-greased mold. Chill in refrigerator until set.

❑ 1 ❑ 2 ❑ 3   651 calories

✢ 23 ✣

For the Party

Calorie counts are not included with these recipes because if you're at a party you don't want to be reminded of them. Live it up. You can go back on your diet tomorrow. Still, most of the recipes in this chapter are reasonably light on calories and, for the most part, are easy to prepare.

The various fish species are pretty much interchangeable so use whatever you have on hand—canned salmon, tuna, or flaked fish left over from some other type of preparation.

CRAB/PIMENTO APPETIZER

3 cans (6 oz.) crabmeat
2 beaten eggs
1 jar (2 oz.) chopped pimento
2 TBsp. diced green pepper
4 TBsp. mayonnaise

1 TBsp. Worcestershire sauce
2 TBsp. Dijon mustard
1 cup fresh bread crumbs
1/4 stick margarine

In a bowl combine all ingredients except bread crumbs and margarine. Spoon 10 to 12 portions into greased individual molds. Pour melted margarine over bread crumbs, sprinkle over crab and bake 30 minutes at 350 degrees.

❑ 1 ❑ 2 ❑ 3

APPETIZER WITH CUCUMBER

1 cup flaked fish	1 TBsp. soy sauce
1/2 cup finely diced cucumber	1/4 tsp. dried dill
2 TBsp. mayonnaise	4-5 drops hot pepper sauce
2 TBsp. sour cream	Salt and pepper to taste

Combine all ingredients, spoon a portion on cracker of your choice, place on a cookie sheet and broil until browned.

❑ 1 ❑ 2 ❑ 3

APPETIZERS WITH CHEESE AND CELERY

1 cup flaked fish	1/2 cup finely diced onion
1 cup grated cheese	4 TBsp. sour cream
1/2 cup finely diced celery	Salt and pepper to taste

Combine all ingredients, spoon a portion on cracker of your choice, place on a cookie sheet and broil until browned.

❑ 1 ❑ 2 ❑ 3

CRAB N' CURRY SPREAD

1 pkg. (8 oz.) cream cheese	1 can (6 oz.) crabmeat
1/4 stick margarine	1/4 tsp. curry powder
1/4 cup diced onion	Salt and pepper to taste

Soften cream cheese and margarine at room temperature or in microwave and combine with remaining ingredients.

❑ 1 ❑ 2 ❑ 3

SALMON SPREAD

1 pkg. (3 oz.) cream cheese	1 TBsp. lemon juice
1/2 cup sour cream	1 TBsp. Worcestershire sauce
2 TBsp. finely diced celery	1 can (7 3/4 oz.) salmon
2 TBsp. diced green onion	Salt and pepper to taste

Combine all ingredients and use as a dip or spread.

❑ 1 ❑ 2 ❑ 3

SALMON DIP WITH CHIVES

1 can (7 3/4 oz.) salmon	*2 TBsp. finely diced onion*
1 cup sour cream	*1 TBsp. parsley flakes*
2 TBsp. lemon juice	*1/4 tsp. garlic powder*
2 TBsp. chives	*Salt to taste*

Combine all ingredients and use as a dip or spread.

❑ 1 ❑ 2 ❑ 3

SMOKED SALMON DIP

1 cup smoked salmon	*2 TBsp. sour cream*
2 TBsp. mayonnaise	*2 TBsp. diced green onion*

NOTE: If you have no smoked salmon use canned salmon and mix in some liquid smoke or smoke flavored salt.

❑ 1 ❑ 2 ❑ 3

DIPPING NUGGETS

Cut fish fillets into one-inch cubes, dip in beaten egg, roll in fine bread or cracker crumbs, deep fry to a golden brown and dip in whatever cocktail sauce or dip you wish.

❑ 1 ❑ 2 ❑ 3

SARA-ANN'S CRAB DIP

1 can cream of celery soup	*1 cup diced green onion*
1 TBsp. plain gelatin dissolved	*1 cup finely diced celery*
in 1/4 cup cold water	*1 cup mayonnaise*
1 pkg. (6 oz.) cream cheese	*1 can (6 oz.) crabmeat*

Combine gelatin with hot soup. Add cream cheese amd stir until well blended. Add remaining ingredients and pour into a well-greased mold. Chill until firm and use as a spread or dip.

❑ 1 ❑ 2 ❑ 3

DILL DIP

1 cup cottage cheese	*1/2 tsp. dried dill*
2 TBsp. lemon juice	*1 cup flaked fish*
2 TBsp. mayonnaise	*1/4 cup chopped pecans/*
	walnuts

Combine all ingredients and use as a dip or spread.

❑ 1 ❑ 2 ❑ 3

SUPER SALMON BALLS

1 pkg. (3 oz.) cream cheese
1/2 stick margarine
1 TBsp, onion flakes
1 TBsp. lemon juice
1 tsp. prepared horseradish

1 tsp. prepared mustard
1 can (7 3/4 oz.) salmon
Salt and pepper to taste
1/2 cup chopped pecans or
  walnuts

After softening the cream cheese and margarine at room temperature or in a microwave, combine with all but the nuts.
Chill in refrigerator to firm up, shape into balls and roll in the nuts.

❑ 1 ❑ 2 ❑ 3

TOMATO HOT SAUCE

1/4 cup diced onion
1/4 cup diced celery
1/4 stick margarine
2 TBsp. flour

1 can (8 oz.) tomato sauce
2 TBsp. chili sauce
1 TBsp. lemon juice
1 tsp. sugar

In saucepan saute onion and celery in margarine until tender. Add
flour, then stir in remaining ingredients until thickened.

❑ 1 ❑ 2 ❑ 3

KWICK KLAM TOMATO DIP

1/4 stick margarine
1 TBsp. flour
3/4 cup tomato juice

1 can (6 oz.) minced clams
Salt and pepper to taste

In a saucepan stir flour into melted margarine. Add remaining
ingredients, stirring until thickened.

❑ 1 ❑ 2 ❑ 3

ONION CLAMATO DIP

1/4 stick margarine
1/2 cup diced onion

1 TBsp. flour
1 cup clam-tomato juice

In a saucepan saute onion in margarine until tender. Stir in flour
and add clam-tomato juice, stirring until thickened.

❑ 1 ❑ 2 ❑ 3

SIMPLE MUSHROOM DIP

1/4 stick margarine
1/2 cup diced onion

1 can cream of mushroom soup
2 TBsp. cornstarch

In a skillet saute onion in margarine until tender, then add mushroom soup. Dissolve cornstarch in a bit of milk and add to soup, stirring until thickened.

❏ 1 ❏ 2 ❏ 3

COCKTAIL SAUCE FOR SHRIMP OR CRAB

3/4 cup chili sauce
1/4 cup lemon juice
1 TBsp. horseradish

1 TBsp. finely diced onion
1 TBsp. Worcestershire sauce
4-5 drops hot pepper sauce

Combine all ingredients and spoon into cups containing shrimp or crab. Best served chilled.

❏ 1 ❏ 2 ❏ 3